TRANSATLANTIC LINERS AT WAR

TRANSATLANTIC LINERS AT WAR

The Story of the Queens

William H. Miller
and
David F. Hutchings

DAVID & CHARLES
Newton Abbot   London

British Library Cataloguing in Publication Data

Miller, William H. (William Henry)
   Transatlantic liners at war: the
   story of the Queens
   1. Transports—Great Britain—History
   —20th century
   I Title   II. Hutchings, D. F.
   359.3′264   UC325.G7

   ISBN 0-7153-8511-9

Typeset by ABM Typographics Limited, Hull
and printed in Great Britain
by Butler & Tanner Limited, Frome and London
for David & Charles (Publishers) Limited
Brunel House   Newton Abbot   Devon

Foreword

Having completed the whole of World War II at sea, I felt that I would never again experience the tensions and anxieties of being at sea in wartime. The two 'Queens' fulfilled a vital role during the years 1939 to 1945 and absolute secrecy was of paramount importance to ensure a safe passage for the ships and all on board.

To find myself in command of *Queen Elizabeth 2* at the time of the Falklands conflict was an unexpected and awesome responsibility. Here was a new concept of war. Electronics and technology had advanced over the intervening years, and secrecy was no longer possible. The sailing from Southampton was televised worldwide, and everyone knew that *Queen Elizabeth 2* was carrying the Welsh Guards, the Scots Guards and Gurkhas to the South Atlantic. As a result, I was very much aware that the ship had become a prime target for the enemy, and that modern communications and satellites could easily reveal her position.

And so I went to war again, thankful for the desolate wastes of the South Atlantic at the onset of winter, and the vast distances which the limited armed forces of Argentina could not hope to cover. The ship's role was notable, in that a large number of highly trained troops had to be taken to the South Atlantic along with their equipment, ammunition and stores. It had to be accomplished quickly, and only one ship could qualify for such a mission. The success of that important venture is now part of maritime history. According to Sir Winston Churchill, the earlier 'Queens' shortened World War II, and so it was that *Queen Elizabeth 2* played her own valuable role in helping to bring the Falklands war to a speedy and successful conclusion.

For my part, I was able to consider ourselves as a portion of that great Task Force, guiding my ship on the 16,000-mile voyage, aware of the hazards and responsibilities of such an essential, unprotected passage.

Queen Elizabeth 2 accomplished all that was asked of her, and it is with pride that her name can truly be remembered and associated with the other great 'Queens'.

Peter Jackson
Master.
Queen Elizabeth 2

Contents

This book is dedicated to the officers and crew members who have staffed the three great Queens and also to Emma and Alexandra

Introduction

On 1 December 1930, at the John Brown shipyards at Scotland's Clydebank, the first hull plates were laid in place for Job Number 534. As one shipyard executive later described the scene: 'It was a particularly raw, foggy winter's day and the electric lights under the cranes of the building berth had to be put on soon after half-past three in the afternoon. However, work continued in the wet and in the darkness well into the night.' Job Number 534 was to be the *Queen Mary*, the first of the legendary Queens, the best-known superliners ever created.

The new ship was being built for the illustrious Cunard Steamship Company Limited of Liverpool, the dominant and periodically most popular liner firm on the Atlantic run to North America. In that crucial year of 1930, just as the world Depression began to grip in earnest, Cunard was running no less than seventeen passenger ships. The new super-Queen was to be the flagship and pride of Britain.

The creation of the *Mary* was the result of extended tests that began in 1926. She was a revolutionary liner; no ship, passenger or otherwise, had been as large or as powerful. Furthermore, while there had been no public mention of a sister-ship or an equivalent running-mate, Cunard was, in fact, thinking of a twin-liner express service to New York. This was to be the first service of its kind, the supreme competitive edge. Even the technologically skilled Germans, with their speedy *Bremen* and *Europa* of the late Twenties, needed a third, companion liner to maintain regular timetables to New York. Cunard as representative of Britain would use only two liners, one sailing each week from alternate sides of the Atlantic. Thus, the *Mary* and her eventual running-mate were designed as large, luxurious hotels that coud make the Atlantic passage in five days. Everything about them, every detail of design and construction, was based on this planned Atlantic relay.

As the Depression heightened and food queues lengthened, the building of the *Queen Mary* became a matter of national pride. However, a year after construction began, in December 1931, she too had a set-back. As Cunard revenues plummeted, shipyard work was suspended. There was even a rumour that the steel shell of the *Mary* would be scrapped on the spot and the project abandoned. Fortunately, just over two years later, the British Government extended loans that allowed work to continue. The construction and completion of the liner became even more symbolic of the national fight for recovery.

On 26 September 1934, Her Majesty Queen Mary went to the Clyde to name the 81,000-tonner at launching. The naming was a tight secret until that very day. It has often been written and repeated that the original choice was *Victoria*. There is a charming, though unfounded, story that suggests that King George V misunderstood Cunard's intentions to name the ship after England's most illustrious queen and thought of his wife and not his grandmother. In fact, *Queen Mary* was the choice almost from the start. It was a thoughtful selection, breaking with the tradition of the recently merged Cunard and White Star Lines' 'ia' and 'ic' (ie *Aquitania* and *Majestic*) nomenclatures. Furthermore, 1935 was to be Silver Jubilee Year, and Queen Mary was a revered icon, herself a symbol to a weary nation.

The *Mary* was completed in the spring of 1936 and the interested public was flooded with details of her creation and size. There were 10,000,000 rivets, 2,000 portholes and windows and a 140-ton rudder that had a door in its side for dry-dock inspections. Also, as anticipated by her builders and owners, she swept the North Atlantic, capturing the prized Blue Riband in August of her maiden year, with a run of 30.6 knots. The French *Normandie* tried to regain the pennant — and finally did so in the spring of 1937. But the *Mary* excelled even further, taking the record permanently in August 1938, with a recorded 31.6 knots.

In those final years of the Thirties, the *Queen Mary* was paired alongside older, large Cunarders such as the *Berengaria* and

Aquitania, that traded between Southampton, Cherbourg and New York. The *Mary*'s running-mate — an even larger, more modern ship — was then still being built at the same Clydebank shipyards. According to Cunard plans, the second superliner would be in service in April 1940. The vision of a two-ship express run, conceived a decade before, would then become a reality.

1

The *Queen Mary* Goes to War

War came early to the *Queen Mary*. Miss Elsie Greenman crossed on the liner in the fateful late summer of 1939, leaving New York on 23 August.

As we sailed from Manhattan, there were ominous rumours of war. From mid-Atlantic, we feared that war had actually been declared as late each afternoon, long before darkness fell, all portholes and windows were blacked-out, and all access to the outer decks blocked. In addition, the BBC news bulletins were replaced by a news summary given over the ship's radio system. We reached Southampton on Monday, August 28th, to discover that war had not yet been declared. Then, most ironically, a full year later, in a suburb of London, I came across a sailor from the battleship HMS *Hood*. I told him of my crossing in the *Mary*. From him, I learned that the *Hood* had shadowed the *Queen* from mid-Atlantic, remaining out of sight over the horizon during daylight hours, but closing in at dusk. The night-time black-out on deck had been for very important security reasons.

The *Mary* sailed westbound from Southampton on 30 August, just two days before the *Luftwaffe* slammed into Poland and shattered world peace. At the same time, in New York, American authorities allowed the *Bremen* to sail for home, but without passengers. In the days ahead, although on far different courses, the British and German liners crossed each other's paths. By the time the *Mary* reached her Manhattan pier and offloaded a record 2,332 passengers, Britain was officially at war. The *Bremen*, repainted in grey disguise during her crossing, went first to Iceland, then Murmansk before cautiously slithering along the Norwegian coastline, dipping in and out of fog-banks and even temporarily hoisting the Soviet colours to avoid capture and attack. She reached Bremerhaven four months later, in December, but was never to sail again. She was laid up, and later destroyed by fire at her pier in March 1941. Her remains were chopped up for the Nazi war effort and the double bottom was later sunk deliberately in the lower reaches of the Weser.

On the south side of New York's Pier 90, and just across from the idle French *Normandie*, the *Mary* waited for her next orders. She was, of course, supposed to return to Southampton according to Cunard's schedule. Instead, the Admiralty told Cunard not to risk the liner at sea and to cancel all her voyages. Her staff was greatly reduced, many of them being sent home to England on other, smaller Cunarders.

As she lay silent, the *Mary* lost her peacetime colours and was repainted in fresh coats of sombre grey. Because she was potentially one of the three largest troop transports, pierside security was extremely heavy. There had been American intelligence reports that Nazi agents in the United States planned to blow her up or set fire to her. Searchlights played along her outer decks, giving a prison-like atmosphere to the night-time operations along Twelfth Avenue. In Britain, a misguided critic, a Member of Parliament, suggested that the liner had no possible wartime use and should therefore be sold to the still-neutral Americans.

Six months later, on 7 March 1940, the *Queen Mary* was joined for the first time by her intended partner and Atlantic running-mate, the *Queen Elizabeth*. The *Elizabeth*, dressed in equally drab grey, arrived following her maiden voyage, a secret dart across the North Atlantic from Scotland. She berthed just across the pier shed from her three-funnelled fleetmate. Together with the *Normandie*, the Cunarders sat in quiet majesty, a haunting splendour, awaiting their calls to duty. The brand-new *Queen Elizabeth* was the largest of the three giants; the *Normandie* was second and assuredly the most luxurious; and the *Mary* was in third place, yet still the world's fastest liner. In a brief comparison:

	Gross tonnage	Overall length	Passenger capacity
Queen Elizabeth	83,673	1,031ft	2,283
Normandie	82,799	1,028ft	1,972
Queen Mary	81,237	1,018ft	2,139

On 1 March 1940, at Liverpool, Cunard was formally told that the *Mary* (and later the *Elizabeth*) was needed for military duty. The reaction was immediate. Nearly 500 crewmembers were sent from another Cunarder, the *Antonia*. A new coat of grey paint was added and most of the twenty-four lifeboats were tested and retested. Although no formal announcement was ever made, deep suspicions were aroused along the Manhattan docks. Fresh supplies were seen being loaded aboard the *Mary*. Then, some two weeks after the *Elizabeth* had first arrived, the *Mary* slipped quietly out of New York harbour. It was the afternoon of 21 March, the formal beginning of her military career. The two Queens would not meet again for a year, when both would be in Australia. As for the *Normandie*, she would never again leave New York harbour. Seized by the United States Government in December 1941, just after the attack on Pearl Harbor, she was converted to a troopship at her West Side pier, the former French Line terminal. A fire broke out on 9 February 1942 and was followed by chaotic, poorly planned firefighting efforts. Overloaded with tons of water, the great liner heeled over and sank at her slip. Her subsequent salvage, which included partial scrapping, took fifteen months and cost over $5 million. Her remains were deemed unusable and the stained and scarred hulk was laid up for a time. After the war ended, the Americans were still uninterested in the scorched shell and she was sold to local scrappers at Port Newark, New Jersey and demolished.

The loss of the *Normandie* was considered a serious blow to the Allied cause. If she had been allowed to sail on the Atlantic GI troop shuttle with the two Queens, her effect would have been extremely significant. The destruction of this French supership, a superbly magnificent creation in her time, prompted many admirals and generals alike to ponder, 'But what if one or both of the Queens were lost as well?' Every precaution, every effort of security, secrecy and safety had to be taken.

The *Mary*, after leaving New York, sped to the South Atlantic under highly secret orders, clinging to the South American coast and then crossing to South Africa. She maintained her peacetime sailing speed of some 28 knots throughout. Just under two weeks later, she

15

put into Cape Town, a port she was surely never expected to visit, appearing quite suddenly, without any public warning, outside the harbour area. Unlike most other liners, the Queens were designed and built only for the North Atlantic express run on a year-round schedule. They were never intended to go elsewhere, not even to cruise occasionally like the *Normandie, Bremen* and *Rex* had done in the late Thirties.

From Cape Town, after refuelling and taking on fresh supplies, the *Mary* sped off, still at an average of 28 knots, across the Indian Ocean. She reached Sydney on 17 April, again a surprise sight in so distant a port. Without ceremony or formal reception, the Cunarder was handled by the yards of Cockatoo Docks & Engineering Company, where she was to be urgently prepared and fully outfitted for war duty — a role she would maintain for over six years.

Within two weeks, extra bunks, toilets, showers and sinks, kitchen facilities and stores were fitted. Many of her fine passenger fittings were removed, coded and listed, packed and sent to Northern Australia for wartime storage. In some areas on board, only the glossy veneers remained, hinting of the suddenly vanished days of peaceful luxury. The soft chairs and sofas, the pylon lamps and the glass bookcases were removed, along with many other items; much of the custom-made china and silver went ashore. The ship was recertified to carry as many as 5,500 troops, an increase of 3,361 over her commercial capacity. It was a stupendous task to convert the world's third largest liner in only fourteen days. Furthermore, the Australians had never seen such a vessel, much less ever handled one of such proportions. Len Houghton was serving aboard the 35,000-ton *Mauretania* at the time: 'We were the first big Atlantic liner to arrive in Sydney and caused great excitement. Everyone wanted to see the *Mauretania*. But when the *Queen Mary* reached the Australian port, we were completely pre-empted.'

On 5 May, with orders in hand to proceed home to England via Fremantle, Cape Town and Freetown, the *Mary* took on over 5,000

The massive bow of the *Queen Mary*, repainted in battleship grey, preparing for military duty in March 1940 (*Frank O. Braynard Collection*)

Australian troops. At Fremantle, she joined one of the war's great troop convoys, consisting of six major former luxury liners: Cunard's four-funnel *Aquitania*, now in her second world conflict; Canadian Pacific's *Empress of Britain* and *Empress of Japan*, the respective flagships of that firm's Atlantic and Pacific passenger operations; and the brand-new *Andes*, the intended flagship for Royal Mail Lines' South American service. Named 'Convoy US3', this fleet — representing over 227,000 tons of valuable troopships — was created to deliver much needed forces to fight the German advances in Europe. The convoy commodore, Captain J. W. A. Waller, was on board the *Empress of Britain*. The group sailed with a naval escort, the cruisers HMAS *Australia*, HMAS *Canberra* and HMNZS *Leander*, for Cape Town and then swung northward to Britain.

Mr N. L. McKellar, then a member of the 2nd Australian Imperial Force, was aboard the *Queen Mary* as a trooper:

I was part of the 6th Australian Division. [The first five divisions had served in World War I.] The division comprised three brigades — the 16th, 17th and 18th. The 16th was mainly raised in New South Wales and sailed from Sydney in what we called the 'First Convoy'. The 17th Brigade was made up mainly of Victorians and sailed from Melbourne as the 'Second Convoy'. The final brigade was made up from Queensland, Tasmania and West Australia, and we comprised the 'Third Convoy'. More officially, these convoys were known as 'US 1', 'US 2' and 'US 3'.

McKellar had come from the outback in Queensland:

Although I had seen ships before, the largest being the 23,000-ton P & O Strath class [*Strathmore, Strathnaver, Strathaird, Strathallan* and *Stratheden*], the *Queen Mary* was absolutely immense, beyond any expectations. It seemed impossible that I and another 4,880 troops would be drafted like sheep through a square hole in the ship's side.

We embarked from Pyrmont on Sydney harbour ferries, which then lay alongside the *Queen Mary*. A soldier going to war has so much equipment hung about him that he looks like a Christmas tree. You can imagine that many of us, with no real experience at this sort of thing, got our rifles, etc caught in the ship's many projections and corners.

'An empress incognito': the brand-new *Queen Elizabeth* racing to New York on her secret maiden voyage (*Frank O. Braynard Collection*)

My initial memories of the *Mary* on that her first trooping trip was that she still had her wine stewards aboard and a magnificent stock of grog and tobacco. The officers on one hand and the warrant officers and sergeants on the other had magnificent messes, with table service and all the frills.

My commanding officer was the senior officer of the *Queen Mary*, who was not, quite curiously, the officer commanding troops. The reason was that we were Army Medical Corps and the OC Troops were artillerymen. My commanding officer had a 'number one' stateroom and, being his right-hand man, I spent much time at the forward end of the main passenger deck. I do not recall it being very hot, not even in the tropics. The rank-and-file, however, did not do so well. Below decks, there were six and eight to a cabin which normally might have held two or three. None the less, the troops took it well. They were allowed on deck both day and night. Of course, there were some who were very worried about getting out if she was torpedoed, but good evacuation plans and plenty of drills ensured that everyone had a good chance. The exceptions, of course, would have been those in the way of any torpedo hit, but then that happened even with small coasters.

McKellar was possibly one of the few soldier-passengers to keep a diary of his southern passage in the *Queen Mary*:

5th May: Weighed anchor 0700 hrs. Circled round outside Sydney Heads until about 1100 hrs. when formed up with convoy. About 1500 hrs. *Mauretania* joined. Convoy then proceeded south. Column positions port: *Empress of Britain* (X3), *Mauretania* (X4), *Andes* (X7); starboard: *Queen Mary* (X1), *Aquitania* (X2), *Empress of Japan* (X6). Turned south 1530 hrs. Escorts HMNZS *Leander*, HMAS *Canberra* and HMAS *Australia*.
6th May: Passed Wilson's Promontory at 1100 hrs. At 1600 hrs. convoy joined by *Empress of Canada* (X5); she took up station as third ship in starboard line, behind *Aquitania* and ahead of *Empress of Japan*. Convoy proceeding due west.
10th May: Arrived off Fremantle. Anchored off Rottnest 1100 hrs. Some vessels went into Fremantle. Australian Naval oiler *Kurumba* alongside 1100 hrs. fuelling.
11th May: Much unhappiness and near-riot aboard *Queen Mary* because no shore leave.
12th May: Weighed anchor 1230 hrs. Course approx. northwest.
13th May: Man overboard from *Aquitania*. Not recovered.
14th May: Man overboard from *Andes*.
15th May: Announced convoy bound for Trincomalee [Ceylon].

16th May: Sea rising. Course changed; announced bound for Cape Town.
20th May: Naval escort changed: HMNZS *Leander* detached. HMS *Shropshire* joined, then HMAS *Canberra* left. HMAS *Australia* remained.
25th May: Heavy zigzagging all day.
26th May: Arrived Cape Town. Anchored 0830 hrs. *Queen Mary*, *Aquitania* and *Empress of Canada* moored offshore; others went into wharves. Tanker *British Chemist* alongside *Queen Mary* 1330 hrs. to 1550 hrs. to bunker. *Queen Mary* moved to Simonstown overnight.
27th May: *British Fortitude* alongside to fuel. Half of the troops on *Queen Mary* granted leave. They went ashore on two flat-bottomed punts towed by local tug.
28th May: Balance of troops allowed leave. Same means of transport ashore. Leave officially from 0800 hrs. to midnight; most troops did not get off *Queen Mary* until 1100 or 1200 hrs.
29th May: Almost all of the troops allowed off yesterday were absent without leave. On the morning of the 29th, Simonstown railway station (the rail service between Simonstown and Cape Town was the only means of communication) was cordoned off by armed troops. Everyone on each incoming train was arrested and conveyed under escort to their ships.
30th May: Men still returning from overstayed leave.
31st May: Left Simonstown weighed anchor 0800 hrs. Noticed that *Empress of Japan* did not join convoy. (After the war, found out that crew refused to sail her.) HMAS *Australia* detached and replaced by HMS *Cumberland*.
7th June: Arrived Sierra Leone (Freetown). Anchored approx. 0700 hrs.
8th June: Weighed anchor 0810 hrs. Proceeded some distance from anchorage, but about 0930 hrs. anchored again; finally got underway at 1700 hrs. HMS *Hermes* joined escort.
10th June: HMS *Hermes* detached.
12th June: HMS *Dorsetshire* joined escort.
14th June: HMS *Dorsetshire* detached; escort reinforced by HMS *Hood*, HMS *Argus* and six destroyers — only the British ones could be identified as HMS *Broke*, HMS *Westcott* and HMS *Wanderer*. Others were RCN.
15th June: About 1100 hrs. passed through a lot of floating debris. About 1200 hrs. sighted ship afire about three miles distant. Air cover provided by Sunderlands. Escort augmented by arrival of HMS *Warwick* and HMS *Witch*. About 1530 hrs. *Queen Mary* scraped some floating object — much noise as the apparent object scraped down the side. No announcement made to say what it was. Round 1800 hrs. passed through a group of drifters apparently sweeping channel.
16th June: Anchored off Gourock 1400 hrs. Sick taken off by steamer *King George V*. HMS *Argus* and HMS *Shropshire* only naval vessels in

sight — both passed *Queen Mary* on opposing course and cheered by troops.

18th June: Disembarked — curiously by *Queen Mary II* [a local steamer].

The call at Simonstown is a particularly vivid recollection for McKellar:

The near-riot at Fremantle was nothing compared to Simonstown. We were supposed to have leave from eight in the morning until midnight. The two punts, which were provided to take us ashore, could carry about 100 men each. You can imagine that getting the men aboard, then the slow tow to the pier, then getting the men off and then slow tow back to the *Queen Mary* meant that by the time that half the leave party had gotten away it was about noon. It is not surprising that most of us — including me — went AWOL. The hospitality of the South Africans was wonderful and we had reckoned that the Army had given us a lousy deal in getting us off the ship as late as two in the afternoon and then wanting us back by midnight. After staying ashore for the night, we caught the train back to Simonstown. As we stepped off the train, we found that the entire station area, yard and every means of access was barred by military and regimental police, all of them with fixed bayonets. We were all arrested. After sailing from Simonstown, it was tabulated that some 2,500 troops were under open arrest. The voyage thereafter was fully occupied with courts martial. All AWOL warrant and non-commissioned officers were reduced in rank. The officers were also court martialled, but because there was no general aboard [a general is needed to confirm the sentencing of an officer], their cases were heard, evidence taken and they were remanded to a field general court martial. In due course, Brigadier General H. C. H. Robertson came aboard. He was not, at that time, in command of the Brigade. We were under the command of Brigadier Morshead who was on another ship. Soon after, it was realised that we were not going to join the other brigades in the Middle East. This reorganisation placed most of us in the 19th Brigade, under the command of General Robertson, who was more commonly known as 'Red Robbie'. When given the command of troops on the *Queen Mary*, Red Robbie — bless his soul — ordered that all disciplinary action against those who went AWOL at Simonstown be cancelled. So everyone either got back their rank or had their fines cancelled.

On 16 June 1940, the *Mary* reached the Clyde, delivering her Australian soldier-passengers. In all, the convoy safely landed 8,000 Australians and a further 6,000 New Zealanders. The Australian troops were stationed first at Salisbury Plain and then at Colchester for the anticipated German invasion of Britain. As for the liner herself, the possibilities of her docking at Southampton were now far too dangerous. The Clyde would be her British base for the remainder of the war.

The *Mary*'s next sailing orders were to the Far East, to deliver forces from Britain to bolster Singapore. She sailed from the Clyde on 29 June, again under highly secret orders, bound for Singapore via the South African Cape. She was again part of an immense convoy, one that variously included: Canadian Pacific's *Empress of Britain* and *Empress of Canada*; Cunard's *Franconia*; Royal Mail's *Andes*; P & O's *Stratheden* and *Strathaird*; Orient Line's *Orion, Otranto* and *Ormonde*; Furness-Bermuda's *Monarch of Bermuda*; Gdynia-America's *Batory*; British India's *Aska*; and the Australian armed merchant cruiser *Kanimbla*, another former liner.

In Commodore Sir James Bisset's enlightening and informative memoirs *Commodore: War, Peace and the Big Ships*, he describes his departure from Gourock in the *Franconia*, along with six other troop-transports, with 3,310 souls aboard — 2,765 soldiers, 87 nurses, 106 civilians and a crew of 352. In all, the convoy sailed 12,000 miles to the Far East, with over 30,000 passengers on board £25 million worth of ships.

At this time rumour was rife that Hitler had offered $250,000 and the Iron Cross with Oak Leaves to the U-boat commander who could sink the *Mary*. Adding fuel to such talk were suspicions that Nazi agents were hard at work, especially in Scotland, to uncover the voyage plans and specific whereabouts of the Cunarder. The *Mary* was guarded more closely than ever. Crewmembers were sworn to absolute secrecy. Those who were loose-lipped, usually in shoreside pubs, promptly found themselves reassigned to duty ashore. Even well-intended Brownie box-camera snaps of the liner were quickly confiscated.

The liner again called at Cape Town and then at remote Trin-comalee on Ceylon before reaching Singapore. On 5 August, after landing her troops, the 1,018-footer was squeezed into that port's naval dry dock, a facility that was never intended to handle so large a vessel. The bow and stern hung over the far ends of the dock boundaries. A forty-one day refit and overhaul commenced, straining manpower and supplies for miles. A new minesweeping paravane system was added, which gave the ship greater protection against underwater mines. This complemented her degaussing strip, which offered additional protection from mines. Her machinery was also overhauled, her hull scraped and yet another new coat of grey paint applied. Between 1940 and 1942, the *Mary* was also fitted with one 4-in gun plus several World War I vintage Lewis and Vickers machine-guns.

The Italian invasion of Egypt in mid-September 1940 created yet another emergency. All possible Allied reinforcements were needed, especially since there was the danger that the Suez Canal might be taken. The *Mary*'s refit was promptly accelerated and the ship ordered to Sydney 'with the greatest possible speed'. She arrived back in Australia on 25 September, but was given three weeks further refit so as to increase her troop capacity even further. Now she was to start her military duty on the Indian Ocean shuttle. Although the *Mary* would sometimes sail without a convoy or warship escort, she was allowed no further west than Bombay or Trincomalee. For her, at this time, the Red Sea and Suez were far too dangerous. She would deliver her urgently needed troops, who would then be transferred to smaller, presumably less valuable ships for the remainder of the journey.

She left Sydney on 20 October and, after a call at Fremantle, went to Bombay, where she arrived for the first time on 26 October. On the following troop voyage, she went to Trincomalee, with an eventual return to Sydney on 24 January 1941. In February, she went back to Singapore for a one-week overhaul and dry-docking.

At the end of March 1941, she made a round trip run between Sydney and Fremantle, following which it was decided finally to extend her voyages all the way to Suez. At the same time, the *Queen Elizabeth* had at last joined the war effort, having left New York the previous November and been outfitted at Singapore. The two Queens met for the second time off Sydney Heads on 9 April, the first of a number of encounters to follow. Both were part of the Indian Ocean troop shuttle and were supported by such other liners as the

Aquitania and *Mauretania* of Cunard, the *Nieuw Amsterdam* of Holland-America and the *Île de France* of the French Line, which was under P & O management for her Eastern service.

The *Mary* left Sydney on 9 April and from Jervis Bay two days later, before proceeding to Fremantle, Trincomalee and then Port Suez on 3 May. Her subsequent trips followed similar itineraries, placing the liner at Suez on 25–26 July, 23–24 September and 22–23 November. These were particularly tense voyages. German submarines and surface craft created an almost constant nerve-racking alert. Furthermore, the sweltering Indian Ocean sun turned the un-air-conditioned Queens into floating infernos, particularly in their lower deck quarters. Temperatures frequently reached well over 100°F. Several soldiers died of heat exhaustion in that blistering summer of 1941. Tempers often flared, strong arguments erupted and there were even cases of rival gang warfare. One cook was shoved into his own heated oven. Hosing the men down, by the security personnel, often dispelled the nastier incidents. Another preventative measure was salt-water showers. The crowded, seemingly inhuman conditions created several near-mutinies. However, by November, at the time of the *Queen Mary*'s final run from Australia to Suez, the two Queens had safely delivered over 80,000 Anzacs to Egypt. In return, they carried many Italian prisoners-of-war to internment in Australia. The good work of the Queens was one of the strong considerations that prompted many Allied leaders to think that 1942 would be a turning point in the war.

Twelve days after the Japanese attack on Pearl Harbor, on 19 December 1941, the *Queen Mary* was ordered to return to New York. Australia itself was now in almost desperate need of reinforcements. The *Mary* arrived at Cape Town from Trincomalee three days after Christmas and, after taking on fuel and supplies, set course for Trinidad, at an average speed of 22 knots. She finally docked at New York's Pier 90 on 12 January 1942 and remained there for a further twelve days. She was then moved to Boston and put into that port's big naval dry dock for a thirteen-day refit. The ill-fated *Normandie*, under American colours as the USS *Lafayette*, had been due to follow her to the Massachusetts port.

When Winston Churchill and his staff visited President Roosevelt in late December 1941, one of the major decisions reached was that the Cunard Queens should carry troops to reinforce the Australian and Pacific fronts against Japanese advances. Therefore, the *Mary*'s capacity and wartime capabilities had to be further increased and improved. At Boston, work crews were loaned from Bethlehem Steel's Quincy shipbuilding yard, who increased the troop capacity from 5,500 to 8,500. Standee bunks were placed in every conceivable area: former lounges, along the enclosed promenades and even in the former first-class suites. Additional lavatory and shower facilities were added. The liner's storerooms and manifests had to be increased to handle over four times her intended capacity. Her artillery was also strengthened with ten 40-mm cannons in five double mounts placed fore and aft, twenty-four single-barrel 20-mm cannons along the upper superstructure, six 3-in high flow angle guns (two on the well-deck forward and four near the fantail aft) and then four very antiquated 2-in anti-aircraft rocket launchers placed next to the third, aft funnel.

The *Mary* took on her next load of troops, 8,398 in all, mostly in the night hours of 17 February 1942. The loading of such high numbers of military passengers, in the secrecy and confusion of darkness, had become common practice in the war years. John Gleason, now a retired New York City businessman, recalled receiving his overseas embarkation orders in December 1943:

We were sent to Fort Hamilton in Brooklyn, at the outer end of New York harbour, and waited there until dark. Then we were placed aboard a ferry, where the windows and portholes were over-painted. I think we went to a pier in Hoboken, but actually we had no true way of knowing. We stepped from the ferry, walked across a narrow pier and then boarded the waiting troopship. We had absolutely no idea what ship we were boarding or, for that matter, where we were headed. I was assigned to B deck and sent their immediately. The bunks were five high with 18in between them. Luckily, I had the top bunk. We set sail in the dark hours as well, but with great confusion. There were mixed units aboard: the air corps, the artillery, some infantry and the MRU (Machine Records Unit). There were about 10,000 of us in total. I was in the older group (late twenties and thirties), but some others were as young as nineteen. It was not until the first daylight that word spread that we were, in fact, aboard the French *Île de France*.

After loading her troop-passengers the *Mary* took on fuel and provisions, and on 18 February, she set sail for Australia via Key West, Rio, Cape Town and then Fremantle and Sydney. Since both Queens had steaming ranges limited to approximately 4,000 miles each, and in an extreme emergency to an absolute maximum of 6,000 miles, neither of them was capable of making exceptionally long distances, for instance direct from New York to Cape Town, without stopping for fuel and provisions, which included fresh water. (The fresh-water situation was a serious consideration throughout the war since both Cunarders were far exceeding their intended capacities. The demands for drinking, cooking and washing water were obviously very high.)

As the *Mary* sped south along America's East Coast, guarded by relays of US Navy cruisers, destroyers and air patrols, intelligence reports were causing concern. Long-range U-boats, fuelled in mid-ocean by large submarine tankers known as 'milch cows', were reportedly bound for the western Atlantic and Caribbean. In particular, Trinidad was among their destinations, earlier proposed as a port-of-call for the *Mary*. Although the level of secrecy was extreme, it was obviously difficult to keep the movements of the Queens completely classified. For example, a call at a tiny island such as Trinidad meant weeks of preparation — for 6,000 tons of fuel, 4,000 tons of fresh water and hundreds of tons of foodstuffs. To dockers, harbour authorities and other interested locals, such staggering preparation meant that one of 'the Monsters' was due. Word could reach the Germans with relative ease. The risks, especially in February 1942, were enormous. In response, orders were flashed to the *Mary* to divert to Key West, Florida.

The liner was safely refuelled and replenished off the Florida port at an anchorage some twenty-three miles at sea. Her new master, Captain James Bisset, was delivered to her by Navy tug and upon seeing her at anchor (resting in 60 ft of water) for the first time, an outline in a faint mist, he found the liner to resemble 'a great rock set in the middle of the sea'. Two 6,000-ton tankers were secured to each side of the *Mary*, both feeding her with much needed supplies. Two US Navy destroyers circled her continuously, assuring protection against a stray or brazen U-boat. Thousands of American servicemen lined her upper, open decks. When she finally departed on 24 February, her logs showed 8,398 troops and 905 crew aboard, a total of 9,303, which was then the greatest number ever embarked in a single vessel. Later, that figure would be well surpassed, by the *Mary* herself.

The proposed call at Trinidad had been sensibly abandoned. The risks were quite justified as ten ships, mostly tankers, had been hit by U-boats on the very course that would have been used by the *Mary*. Instead, racing at 30 knots, she swung around the western end of Cuba and then headed easterly off the Virgin Islands. High speed and constant zigzagging were her prime defences against possible attack. She could even outpace a torpedo, except when fired at very close range; the speed of a torpedo could rarely exceed 30 knots.

An SOS distress call was received from a torpedoed, sinking tramp in the eastern Caribbean, but the *Mary* could only sail onward. Throughout the war, she was under the strictest orders never to stop, not even for a man overboard, or to answer distress calls. Always, she was to maintain her high speed and prescribed course.

The *Queen Mary* reached Rio on 6 March, anchored again in the outer harbour and was fed by tankers and small craft moored alongside. Rarely during the war years did either of the Queens actually dock at a pier, with the obvious exception of New York. Even at Gourock, their British base for the duration of hostilities, they remained at anchor. The possibility of quick escape, among other reasons, was essential. At anchor, however, the Queens always needed at least three-quarters of a mile for swing space as well as a minimum of 45 ft in depth.

When the Germans learned of the *Mary*'s presence at Rio, a radio report from Berlin suggested that she would be sunk upon leaving. She did, in fact, sail at dusk on 8 March, in complete black-out. Several days later, Japanese radio reported that she had been sunk in the South Atlantic. Captain Bisset was told of the report by his wireless officer and supposedly replied, 'Don't let the troops know that we've been sunk. It might worry them.' The *Mary* sped for South Africa.

During this southern transit, a serious fire lasting two hours erupted in a companion on B deck, just below the bridge section. It was caused by a fault in the electrical insulation, prompting considerable tension among the alerted officers. The ship was 1,500 miles from shore and totally unescorted. The section was sealed off and, although smoke and fumes rose to the bridge level, everyone performed perfectly. Both crew and troops had been instructed not only in emergency boat drill but in fire drill as well. Quite dissimilar from ordinary peacetime passengers, these disciplined men avoided any sense of panic and alarm.

At Cape Town, in the shadows of the magnificent Table Mountain, the *Mary* was joined for the remainder of the voyage by Sir Thomas Blamey, Commander-in-Chief of the Australian Army, and his wife. Lady Blamey found herself to be the only woman on board, in company with 9,304 men! The passage across the Indian Ocean to Fremantle took eight days, at an average speed of 25 knots. Outside that port, the liner was met by two US Navy escort cruisers, the USS *Barker* and USS *Bulwer*. She loaded another 6,000 tons of fuel and 2,000 tons of fresh water before sailing on to Sydney.

Frank Bilek, who had enlisted in the US Air Force just six weeks before, was on board that sailing from Boston to Australia:

We had come down from a camp in Bangor, Maine and boarded the *Mary* under great secrecy at Boston. She was completely blacked-out; the portholes and windows were all covered over. Later, we learned that we were bound for Java, in the South Pacific, by way of South America and South Africa. We were to have gone out in the *Normandie* from Boston, but, of course, she had just burned and capsized at New York. The plans were changed. Instead, the *Mary* would take us and we would be the first American troops to use the Cunarder.

We boarded late in the afternoon of the 17th [February] and then sailed at about noon on the following day. As we ate in that big dining room, the portholes were opened, and we could smell the salt air. We sped south, to the Caribbean, without an escort. Of course, the *Mary* rolled a great deal. [The *Queen Mary* was always a rather notorious roller. It was often said that she could roll the milk out of a cup of tea.]

Bilek recalled the stopovers during this tense voyage:

During the refuelling stop off Key West, we were so far at sea that we couldn't see Florida. Then, at Rio, we were anchored alongside both

German and Japanese ships, since Brazil was then still a neutral nation. Afterward, at sea, bound across the South Atlantic, we intercepted a message that a 'wolf pack' of twenty-five Nazi subs were waiting for us. We were very fortunate to speed off in safety.

Life on board was quite different from the peacetime days:

We did have use of some of the staterooms. [The ship was not yet completely fitted with extensive standee troop berths.] The two indoor pools were still in use and these were diversions. We washed in salt water, using special soap that made suds. We ate in the former dining rooms, which had been converted to mess halls. Only the original panel walls and some of the art work remained. All of the original tables, chairs, china and silverware had been removed. Instead, we sat on long benches, before long tables and ate off Army trays.

Bilek recalled the fire, which had hit in southern waters:

Of course, we could smell the smoke, even down below. The alarms sounded and the ship was slowed to 3 knots. This all hit between two and three in the morning. We were prepared to 'abandon ship', but fortunately that never happened.

Once we reached Australia, we put into Fremantle. Even at this late stage in the voyage, our final destination was still a secret. Rumour was that we would go direct to Java. In our manoeuvrings, off the Australian coast, we somehow misjudged and were caught in a mine field at that. The local pilot boat was summoned and it gently guided us out. Then, after circling about for three days, we went to Sydney, our final call. We were loaded into harbour ferries and sent ashore. It was the last time that many of us would see the *Mary* until well after the war.

The *Mary* reached Australia's biggest port on Saturday, 28 March, concluding the thirty-four-day voyage from Boston. She anchored at Athol Bight, just off the city's zoo, at 6.30pm and immediately began offloading her troops into harbour ferries, which came directly alongside. Once ashore, these troops were bussed to camps outside Sydney. The disembarkation of over 8,300 military personnel was completed by 1am, concluding the arrival of the first contingent of American troops to bolster the defences of Australia. Singapore had just fallen to the Japanese six weeks before and was followed by the collapse of Java, Timur and New Guinea. An Australian invasion was thought to be imminent, but some of her best fighting men were away, serving on other fronts, including North Africa and Britain itself.

After nine days in port, the *Mary* was ordered to return to New York via Fremantle, Cape Town and Rio. She sailed on 6 April, loaded with 832 crewmembers and a mere 58 passengers, and again met the inbound *Queen Elizabeth* just outside Sydney Heads. The *Elizabeth* was delivering the second big contingent of US forces to Australia, although from the West Coast. Despite reports that Japanese submarines were lurking off the Australian coast in wait for the *Mary*, she proceeded safely to South Africa and then went northward to Rio and New York. On 6 May, while some 600 miles south of her American destination, near Bermuda, five lifeboats with survivors from the torpedoed Canadian National passenger ship *Lady Drake* were spotted. Again, the *Mary* could not stop. Instead, the lifeboats' position was reported to the US Navy for rescue. The liner continued on and safely reached her Manhattan dock on 7 May.

Then, quite suddenly, in a change of orders, the *Queen Mary* was reassigned to the North Atlantic, to the famed 'GI shuttle'.

2
The *Elizabeth*, an 'Empress Incognito'

Although almost always thought of as a pair of sister ships, the two Cunarders were quite different from each other. Most obvious, the *Queen Mary* was a three-funneller with rather cluttered upper decks (deckhouses, ventilators, blowers, and so on) whereas the *Elizabeth* had two funnels and a far cleaner upper deck arrangement. Furthermore, the *Mary*'s foredeck had a well whereas the *Elizabeth*'s was flush, supposedly a better design for ocean-going ships. The rake of the *Elizabeth*'s bow was also sharper, in fact far more knife-like. Statistically, the *Mary* was the slightly smaller — at 81,237 gross tons and 1,018 ft overall — yet presumably the faster as she alone held the Blue Riband (1938–52). The *Elizabeth* was never officially 'pushed' to her absolute maximum speed and thus it remains unclear whether or not she was, in fact, equal to or faster than her running-mate. She was, however, the largest liner ever built, at 83,673 tons. Her 1,031 ft was exceeded by only one other liner, the 66,348-ton *France* of 1962, which measured a full 4 ft longer.

While the *Queen Mary* broke new ground in ocean liner construction, the design and creation of the *Queen Elizabeth* had the enormous advantage of the considerable research and early experience not only with the *Mary*, but such other Atlantic superliners as the *Bremen*, *Europa*, *Rex*, *Conte di Savoia* and *Normandie*. There was no official press announcement on this second Queen until as late as February 1936, a mere three months before the *Mary*'s maiden voyage to America. There was indeed ample time for testing, research, comparisons, improvements and serious fact-finding with the *Mary*, and even some disguised spying aboard the innovative *Normandie*.

The second Cunarder would ply the same five-day North Atlantic express run between Southampton, Cherbourg and New York. She would use the same specially built piers at all ports as well as the new King George V Graving Dock at Southampton for overhauls. While creating the *Mary* had been a far-reaching, lengthy affair, efforts for the *Elizabeth* were less exhaustive.

Selecting a name for this new giant was also something of a mystery. The *New York Herald Tribune* of 16 December 1936, and on several occasions thereafter, confidently predicted that she would be named *King George V*, in deference to the late King. It seemed a fitting selection. However, it was not until February 1938, that Cunard announced that *Queen Elizabeth* was the selection. They simply chose to honour the new Queen of England. A few months later, the first sketches of the liner were released. For the first time, the public saw that she was to be a twin-funneller and quite different from the *Mary*.

Both George VI and Queen Elizabeth were due at the launching ceremonies at the John Brown shipyards at Clydebank that were set for 27 September 1938. However, because of the pressing political situation in Europe, the King had to cancel at the last moment. The Queen, accompanied by the Princesses Elizabeth and Margaret Rose, named the liner as planned in the presence of 500,000 spectators. Soon after, the newly christened *Queen Elizabeth* went to an adjacent fitting-out dock, systematically surrounded by 100 concrete blocks that were laced together to prevent the liner from grounding herself on the Clydeside mud.

A year later, on 16 September 1939, both the King and Queen were expected to tour the nearly complete liner at the shipyards, just seven months prior to the projected maiden voyage from Southampton on 24 April 1940. The royal visit never occurred. A little more than two weeks before, the Germans invaded Poland and war had begun. Work on the *Elizabeth* came to a sharp halt. All attention at the John Brown yards was turned instead to far more urgent military orders: for battleships, cruisers and destroyers. For two months, the new Cunarder sat quietly. Then, on 2 November, the Ministry of Shipping in London granted a special licence to resume the fitting-out, but only for important plumbing and electrical work.

None of the passenger accommodation was to be fully completed. The government exemption was prompted by two most important reasons: freeing the shipyard pier space as soon as possible for more pressing warship work and also to move the ship to a safer location, namely New York. Cunard management, together with the Admiralty, felt that the liner was under serious threat, either as a target for sabotage or, more likely, an air attack by the *Luftwaffe*. New York became the secret destination; very few were to know of this.

The *Elizabeth* was ordered away from the Clyde on 6 February 1940, by the express command of Winston Churchill, then First Lord of the Admiralty. An elaborate disguise was created. It was made known publicly that the liner would first go to Southampton, a seemingly logical decision. Stores clearly marked 'Southampton' were loaded aboard, some internal fittings were sent ahead to the southern port and even the King George V Graving Dock was prepared for the vessel. John Havers, a Southampton ship enthusiast and soldier then posted to the Southampton Docks, remembers the scheme: 'We were absolutely convinced that she was coming. We had visions of that day when she would sail along the Solent and eventually go into the graving dock.'

Painted in dismal grey and with many of her lifeboats missing (to lighten the ship for the sensitive run along the often shallow Clyde), the liner left her Clydebank fitting-out berth on 26 February, three weeks after Churchill's order. Just days before, a coded message was flashed to Cunard's New York office to clear the north side of Pier 90, just across from the idle *Queen Mary*, now also in grey warpaint. In response, the smaller *Mauretania* was moved out of the needed slip and redocked at Pier 86, four blocks south. But still,

The first meeting of the great Queens: crewmen stand on the stern of the *Mary*, berthed at Pier 90, as the *Elizabeth* arrives in the Hudson River for the first time on 7 March 1940 (*Frank O. Braynard Collection*)

The *Mary* photographed on 19 March 1940, two days before her first sailing as a troopship. The stores in the foreground were to be loaded aboard the ship and the different shades of grey along the hull were to be matched prior to departure (*Frank O. Braynard Collection*)

there was great secrecy. Only a few hundred people noticed the *Elizabeth* as she moved along the lower reaches of the Clyde, a far different number and mood than when tens of thousands had gathered cheerfully to send off the *Mary* just four years earlier.

Safely manoeuvred by tugs, the *Elizabeth* reached the end of the river and anchored at the Tail of the Bank. She was promptly but unceremoniously handed over to Cunard, in a brief transaction in the intended tourist-class restaurant, with a precedent-breaking lack of trial runs and tests. A special crew had to be gathered, taken mostly from the *Aquitania*, for what was expected to be the coastal voyage to Southampton. Then, during an early boat drill, they were told that the liner was, in fact, going to sea, her final destination still unknown. Several fearful members signed-off at the last moment. Others demanded an extra £50 in safety compensation. Rumour was that she would dash for Halifax. Even the final Scottish pilot was ordered to stay aboard and sail with the liner, travelling with nothing more than an extra pocket handkerchief.

Under misty skies, the *Queen Elizabeth* began her secret maiden voyage at 7.30am on 2 March. Escorted by four destroyers and some aircraft overhead, she immediately began steaming at over 26 knots, heading westward across the Irish Sea. With a greatly reduced crew (finally counted at 398) that had little familiarity with the new vessel, she had scarcely any protection on board. At best, there was a pair of pillboxes on the bridge and aft end, and some sandbags. She maintained strict radio silence and was blacked-out.

One engineer later described life on this secretive westward passage:

There were no carpets aboard, just the bare steel floors, no heating and the light fittings were just hanging wires. There were miles of electric cable all over her, unconnected to anything. And, what was most important, her launching gear had not been removed and this meant additional drag on her speed. Normally, this would have been removed in dry dock.

Elizabeth at anchor in Narrows, New York, after her secret dash for safety (*Everett Viez Collection*)

There was little radio contact as the ship continued to plough west, except one message to alter course and avoid a convoy. She was making a quick escape, something of a dramatic royal exile, and her movements and course had to remain top secret. Even those on board were still unsure of her ultimate destination. She became the 'phantom ship'. As she neared North America, one of her crew finally broke radio silence and overheard a BBC broadcast that said the liner was headed for New York. The secrecy had ended at last.

Even with her name painted over by grey paint, the *Elizabeth* could not be mistaken when she reached New York on 7 March, being first spotted by a TWA aeroplane off Fire Island. Riding high out of the water, she was safely alongside Pier 90 by late afternoon. For the first time, the two Queens were in sight of one another. The idle *Normandie*, on the north side of adjoining Pier 88, completed the awesome trio. At Cunard's New York Office, a message was received: 'I send you my heartfelt congratulations on the safe arrival in New York of the *Queen Elizabeth*. Ever since I launched her in that fateful year of 1938, I have watched her progress with interest and admiration. Please convey to Captain Townley my compliments on the safe conclusion of her hazardous maiden voyage. Elizabeth R.' Churchill wired: 'Splendid! Very good indeed! I never had any doubt about getting her over.'

Cunard had asked for no publicity. Only official visitors were allowed on board and guards surrounded Pier 90. No harbour welcome was accorded other than the customary whistle salutes between ships and the fleet of tugs needed for the final docking. However, the morning papers dutifully recorded the arrival, often with a series of aerial photos of the ship proceeding along the Hudson. The *New York Post* dramatically called her 'an empress incognito, grey-veiled for her desperate exploit'.

Ralph Freeman, a New Yorker transplanted from his native Britain by the threat of war, recalled the arrival of the *Elizabeth*:

A morning paper ran the headline: LINER *ELIZABETH* OFF NANTUCKET APPROACHING NEW YORK. I read those dramatic words at an upper-Broadway news-stand. I was a student at Columbia at the time and resolved to see the arrival. The difficulty was to guess the time for the British weren't that co-operative about those things. I could only skip classes and wait at the Battery, peering down the Lower Bay. At last, through the mist of light snow flurries on that brisk March morning, a great mass congealed on the horizon. There she was! What a thrill that this daring task had succeeded. At first, I thought of scurrying for the next Staten Island ferry. But something stayed me while I calculated speeds and distances in my head. Just as well, for the ferry I caught met her just off the Statue of Liberty. The ferry whistled a frenzied welcome but the *Queen* did not respond. She slid by in silent majesty. Her sombre gray told the reason.

The escape voyage had worked. The Germans were furious. *Luftwaffe* planes, perched above Southampton on the expected date of the *Elizabeth*'s arrival, finally departed in frustration. When the liner eventually reached the safety of New York, Nazi radio sharply responded that the British could no longer trust the safety of their own ports.

Cunard arranged for the appropriate completion of the *Elizabeth* at New York: the plumbing and electrical fittings were fully installed, the heating system finished, full life-saving equipment added, telephones and radios put aboard and the ventilation system overhauled. Much of the work was done by relay teams of workers from the Todd shipyards across the Hudson in Hoboken. While most of the *Elizabeth*'s crewmembers returned home aboard the *Scythia*, the ship remained, seemingly lifeless under her grey coat, along the West Side of Manhattan. Later, she was moved from the north side of Cunard's Pier 90 to the south berth of the same 1,100-ft long finger pier. She was maintained by a small maintenance staff and used only a single boiler, generating just enough power to run her pumps, heating system and necessary lighting.

Throughout the summer of 1940, only 'necessary, civilian completion work' was carried out on the *Elizabeth*. Absolutely no wartime preparations could be made, which could seriously blemish American neutrality. The *Elizabeth* was, of course, the subject of considerable rumour, a myriad of part truths and exaggerations. Sunday supplements often outlined detailed schemes of how such big liners might best serve the war effort. Probably the most persistent rumour surrounding the *Elizabeth* was a proposal to partially remove her upperworks and convert her to a combination aircraft carrier-troop-ship. Theories put forth included creating a balanced capacity for 48 aircraft and 6,000 troops or, far more elaborately, gutting most of her innards for 270 aircraft and only a mere handful of service personnel. Cunard was said to be understandably very much against such plans. The thought of vastly gutting and then rebuilding Britain's brand-new merchant flagship prompted strong protest from Liverpool to both London and Washington. 'Never!' was the response of one company official.

In mid-September, at a special conference held in New York between Cunard and the British Ministry of Shipping, it was decided that the *Elizabeth* would follow the *Mary* and become a high-capacity troop-carrier. Again, the decision was highly secret, even as the final details were worked out. A month or so later, it was firmly agreed that she would go first to Singapore, appropriate British territory and where one of the few capable dry docks was available. Like the *Mary*, she would follow the same routing: to the South Atlantic, then around the South African Cape and finally across the Indian Ocean. Beyond the dry-docking, it was further decided that she would go to Australia, for final outfitting as a troopship and then join the *Mary* and others on the Sydney-to-Suez shuttle.

New York's Twelfth Avenue waterside was buzzing with rumours in those weeks prior to the *Elizabeth*'s departure. On 9 October, over a month prior to her sailing, at least one Manhattan newspaper suggested that:

... despite the strict guard, hundreds of mattresses have been taken aboard, giving support that the liner would soon be a transport. A week ago, the Cunarders *Scythia* and *Samaria* brought 190 more seamen to augment the 143 men left on the larger boat. Another liner is expected this week with more crewmembers. There have been rumors that the British Admiralty has asked the US Navy for permission to dry dock the *Queen* at the Boston Navy Yard in order to scrape her bottom before sending her on sea duty.

On 8 November, there were still further press reports and rumours: 'More crewmen for the *Elizabeth* arriving by bus from Canada, tons of supplies being loaded onboard.'

Three days later the *Herald Tribune* reported:

Renewed bursts of activity aboard the *Queen Elizabeth*, the world's largest liner, today brought predictions on the waterfront that the Cunard-White Star liner would slip quietly out to sea within the next twelve to forty-eight hours. The tempo of preparations was so spirited that it was believed that possibly the ship would leave its berth at the foot of West 50th Street some time tonight on high tide. High tide strikes Governors Island at 6.06pm.

It is known that the British Government plans to use the vessel as a troopship. She would sail from here under sealed orders. Each of the ship's twenty-six lifeboats were being loaded with food, water, lifebelts and other equipment today. On the starboard side, thirteen lifeboats were lowered into the water to test their seaworthiness. A heavy police detail guarding the giant liner and the *Normandie*, next door at West 48th Street, barred all from approaching the ship except the regular crewmembers and new sailors arriving by bus from Canada.

Two days later, the *Elizabeth* finally made her departure. The *Tribune* reported the event:

The *Queen Elizabeth* ended eight months of idleness yesterday [13 November] and put to sea under a drizzling rain. There was no ceremony about the departure. Members of her complement of 465 — not including six sailors who were discharged and left behind for some unspecified acts of rowdiness — professed ignorance as to their next ports of call. Some of them thought that the *Queen Elizabeth* would go first to Trinidad or Halifax.

The *Queen Elizabeth* sailed at 3.32pm. The red duster of the British Merchant Marine drooped from her main gaff. The heavily-loaded, grey-camouflaged ship drew thirty-eight-and-a-half feet forward and forty-one feet aft. With the aid of three tugs, she took advantage of dead slack water on a low tide. She gave a series of warning whistles. Then, when the electric traffic light atop the river-end of the West 50th Street Pier changed from red to green, indicating that the Hudson was free of traffic, her lines were cast off.

Fewer than 200 persons saw her edge away from the pier. Two mounted policemen and a score of foot patrolmen kept newspapermen and photographers outside 'the restricted zone' signs thirty feet from the pier. The ship performed a semi-circle in the Hudson and then headed seaward. Two Coast Guard patrol boats and a marine police boat trailed the ship to the outer harbor.

Once at sea — blacked-out, with radio silence and racing at a prescribed zigzag course — the *Elizabeth* headed for Trinidad, where preparations were already under way for her to load 6,000 tons of fuel oil and 4,000 tons of fresh water. Ideally, she might have gone direct to South Africa, but, like the *Mary* before her, she was designed only for the North Atlantic express run of five to six days. Few could have ever envisioned such far-flung wartime voyages.

On 27 November, the *Elizabeth* reached Cape Town and anchored in the outer harbour. A crewman from the American liner *President Garfield*, then still on a neutral world-cruise run, snapped a photo of the waiting Cunarder. A month later his scene appeared in several New York newspapers. However, by then there was little danger. The *Elizabeth* had already reached Singapore and begun her phase in dry dock. Her exact movements were still clouded, however. On 21 December, the *New York Daily News* reported that both the *Elizabeth* and *Mary* were at Bombay, taking on thousands of Italian prisoners, who had been relayed from Egypt for internment in Australia. In reality, only the *Mary* had been to Bombay.

The welcome at Singapore for the *Elizabeth* was not the warmest. Apart from straining manpower and supply forces for miles around, some of the crew from the *Mary*, which had been there in August, had left a poor impression. It seemed that several, overcome by the boredom of the long dry dock call had been rowdy and disturbing; one group practically demolished a local pub. The *Elizabeth* used the sole large government graving dock at Singapore, just as the *Mary* had done four months earlier. Her bow and stern sections hung over the far ends of the dock. Over several weeks, the hull was scraped, her engines overhauled, guns were fitted along the upper decks and another fresh coat of grey was applied.

Afterwards, the *Elizabeth* went to Sydney, to begin her full conversion to a troopship. Some Australians were confused, however, amidst the great secrecy. One official was overheard to say, 'Gawd, these English are clever. What camouflage. They've even taken away one funnel!' He, among others, was convinced that the *Mary* had returned with one less funnel. As with the other Cunarder, the task of converting the *Elizabeth* was handled by the Cockatoo Docks & Engineering Company. Among the preparations was the creation of sufficient hospital spaces for the thousands of troops that were to be carried. Wards were erected in parts of the main lounge, smoking room, garden lounge and a special isolation section in the stern area. All beds were placed athwartships, since doctors didn't want patients falling out of bed when the ship was rolling. An X-ray department was fitted in the Turkish baths.

Embarrassed port officials at Sydney admitted that only one of the Queens could be properly handled in the harbour at one time — quite simply, there was not sufficient 'swing space' for both ships at once. Consequently, if one Queen was at Sydney, loading or simply at anchor, the other would have to go to Hobart on Tasmania.

The Queens met for the second time just outside that port, off Sydney Heads, on 9 April 1941. Both were part of a major outbound convoy bound for Suez. Some 5,600 troops were aboard the *Elizabeth* and 6,000 on the *Mary*. A further 4,400 were on the *Mauretania*, which had also joined the Indian Ocean troop shuttle. When the two Queens reached Suez, in early May, it was not only the first time that they were in the Red Sea together, but the first time that they could go unescorted from Aden to Suez. The Italian defeat in Eritrea in April allowed this freedom.

Just as for the *Mary*'s passengers, these Indian Ocean voyages were tense and worrying for those on the *Elizabeth*. German submarines and surface vessels were a serious, constant worry. Then, once again, the elements played their part as well. The intense, furnace-like heat caused several deaths (one slightly exaggerated report said that there were burials at sea every four hours), created numerous arguments, fist fights and mutinous outbursts. Temperatures of 125°F were not uncommon in the lower deck quarters. Often, after calling at Suez and laying at anchor for days, it would take the Queens some forty-eight to sixty hours before lower deck cooling even began; they were never intended for such tropical voyages.

The *Elizabeth* made three troop voyages, each of about six weeks, across the Indian Ocean — taking Australian and New Zealand troops to Suez and then often returning with prisoners-of-war. Like the *Mary*, she had the good fortune never to be attacked, even if enemy intelligence reports were sometimes as close as two days off target on her exact whereabouts. Mostly, she sailed in convoys, wedged between supposedly less valuable tonnage, which greatly cut her sailing speed from 27–28 knots to more moderate and more dangerous figures. Among her companions at this time, the Dutch *Nieuw Amsterdam* could barely make 23 knots while the creaking *Île de France* often strained to make 20.

When the Queens were selected to bring American reinforcements for the defence of Australia, the *Elizabeth* was ordered to the West Coast. She was in need of dry-docking, having last been overhauled nearly a year before at Singapore. But now Singapore was far too dangerous (and, in fact, shortly to fall to Japanese invaders). The alternative dry dock of sufficient capacity was part of a Naval dock-yard at Esquimalt in British Columbia. In early February 1942 the *Elizabeth* made course for western Canada.

A special refuelling rendezvous was arranged at the Marquesas, the tiny French-held Pacific islands. The *Elizabeth* was to meet a US tanker to replenish her fuel supplies for the long voyage. She arrived, sounded her whistles as planned but no tanker appeared; the place seemed deserted. A handful of islanders were seen peering from the shoreline. What a sight the giant, grey *Elizabeth* must have been to them. Then, somehow delayed, the smaller vessel appeared on the horizon; the *Elizabeth* was able to continue.

At Esquimalt, she arrived in early morning, expecting to go straight into dry dock. Instead, her Canadian docking pilot ordered her back to sea, for an unintended 'cruise to nowhere'. She had missed the essential morning tide, because of a miscalculation by her officers, and so had to wait until the following day. Then, there were still more problems. As she finally entered the dry dock, there were some serious damages to the facility itself. Again, someone on board had miscalculated — the anti-mine devices on the bow and along the hull had not been removed and they cut into the dock wall.

After refitting, the *Elizabeth* was ordered to San Francisco, her first and only call to that port, to load her soldier-passengers bound for Australia. There were yet more problems. Soon after arriving, quite near to the Golden Gate Bridge, she went aground briefly. Quickly, extra tugs were summoned to her rescue and then they gently manoeuvred the 83,000-ton hulk back into the proper chan-nel. She sailed from San Francisco on 19 March, loaded with over

8,000 American servicemen and a crew of 875.

After landing their troops in Australia (the *Mary* had delivered some 8,300 from Boston to Sydney via the Cape), the two Queens were ordered to return to New York to assist with the massive transition of American and Canadian forces to Britain. As they made their crucial deliveries of over 16,000 personnel, the Queens met for a third time, on 6 April, again off Sydney Heads. The *Mary* was already outbound, returning to New York; the *Elizabeth* was just arriving from San Francisco. Soon afterwards, the *Queen Elizabeth* — loaded with some civilian passengers — set course for New York from Sydney via Cape Town and Rio. By June, just like the *Mary*, she was now ready for the transatlantic relay of hundreds of thousands of troops and wartime passengers.

3

The World's Largest Troopers

By the spring of 1942, the forces in Europe urgently needed reinforcement. The Cunard Queens were selected to substantially bolster this massive transfer of servicemen from one side of the Atlantic to the other. They were to undertake their most illustrious wartime duty carrying almost mind-boggling numbers on each crossing. No two ships have ever performed as well.

The *Mary* was selected to bring over the first big contingent of Americans to Britain, to launch the 'GI shuttle'. At Pier 90, on the night of 10–11 May, some 9,880 American troops were embarked, which, combined with the crew of 875, would make the first time that over 10,000 souls were to sail in a single ship. The exact final figure was put at 10,755. Once again, the *Mary* used her high speed and zig-zag pattern. She crossed to Gourock in five days, three hours, at an average of 25.5 knots. There had been strong rumours in Britain, as there were with many of the liner's wartime sailings, that the '*Queen Mary* was sunk, taking all hands'. This was a disadvantage of the secrecy which surrounded the two Queens. Such rumours could be neither confirmed nor denied without making the position and movement of the ships known to the enemy. Consequently, there were many tense and anxious moments for the families and friends of passengers and crew. For those believers in tales of disaster, it was often a joyous surprise to see one of the liners arrive safely at the Clyde.

At Gourock, there was yet another flash change of order. The *Mary* was despatched to Suez via the Cape, to reinforce the Allies against Rommel's heavy push from Libya into Egypt and to offset the pressing rumour of a German counter-attack. She sailed without escort or convoy throughout this voyage, with 9,357 troops aboard along with 1,000 tons of military cargo and 1½ tons of British currency for Army payrolls.

46

At Cape Town, as usual, she was refuelled and given fresh provision, but with the serious worry ahead that Japanese submarines were reported to be in the Indian Ocean. Complicating matters further, the *Mary* was to make the entire 6,200-mile passage from the Cape to Suez without any stopovers. She had to have full provisions for ten to twelve days, for her 10,409 passengers and crew — the absolute maximum of her endurance and the longest port-to-port passage ever made by the ship.

She was finally escorted by British and Australian naval vessels in the Gulf of Aden, the Red Sea and then in the Gulf of Suez. Just as with her earlier Indian Ocean voyages, the *Mary* and her complement had to endure appalling conditions in the notorious June heat as well as a severe sandstorm. Three men perished of heat prostration. Emergency salt-water showers were erected along the lower decks, troops were allowed to sleep on deck at night and the air-conditioned barber shop, the only such cooled space on board, was used as a special emergency ward. Once at Port Said, her troops were loaded into Nile River barges and ferries and sent ashore. Soon they would be involved in the battle of El Alamein.

The *Mary* left Suez on 23 June 1942, for New York via the Cape and Rio. On this voyage, she carried a diverse assortment of 2,565 souls: 1,398 German prisoners-of-war, 300 Polish guards, groups of Navy, Army and Air Force troops, and some women and children. Then, once again safely at New York, she was ordered to the Clyde, sailing on 2 August. With 15,125 troops aboard plus 863 crew, creating a final figure of 15,988, this total was far and away the greatest yet taken in a single vessel. Furthermore, it marked the first time that an entire US division was travelling in one ship.

The *Queen Mary* (and *Queen Elizabeth*) had been freshly fitted with 12,500 standee berths, positioned in every conceivable space from the former main lounge to the tourist-class smoking room. She was also certified under wartime dispensations to take an additional 3,500 troops, described as 'overload' passengers, who could sleep on the decks during summer crossings. The standee bunks, an American creation, were made of tubular steel, to which were attached strips of canvas stretched with rope lacings. According to the height of the area, three or more bunks could be fitted in one tier. During the day, they could be hinged upward and secured to the bulkhead with a small chain and hook lock. They were very sensible and adequate creations: lightweight, easily cleaned and had no crevices to conceal vermin. Such bunks were often used in rotation, sleeping three servicemen in a trio of eight-hour shifts.

Every available space was considered precious and put to good use. The only parts of the ships which were left clear and untouched were the alleyways and companionways. Only two dining rooms and two lounges were retained to provide eating and recreation spaces. Even the two indoor swimming pools were made into mess halls and the squash courts into stores.

The Queens were the two mainstays of the convoys which set out to reinforce the 8th Army. Between December 1942 and April 1943, when both ships worked the North Atlantic, they carried a total of 105,000 troops and steamed 339,000 miles. The state of the war had made it possible for the two ships to perform the duty for which they were originally intended — crossing and re-crossing the North Atlantic. For every eastbound voyage, a whole division of infantry could be taken into the battle zone.

The *Elizabeth* made thirty-one wartime transatlantic round trips between Gourock and New York, and three to Halifax. Although specific details certainly varied, the general operations of the two Queens were quite similar for their war service.

Captain Eric Ashton-Irvine served aboard the *Elizabeth* as a junior officer in 1942 (and later aboard the *Mary* in 1944–45):

The weather on the North Atlantic between New York (or Halifax) and Gourock was usually filthy. There were fogs, gales, freezing rains, snows and sleets. In the deepest fogs, we sailed direct, as if under a guarded curtain, for the shores of Scotland. Otherwise, we zigzagged and always constantly. Of course, we could never have, nor expect, any form of escort. We were simply too fast (averaging 28 knots and sometimes better). At best, the underwater U-boats could make 7–8 knots. Even in the worst weather, we could still do 18–19 knots. In home waters, even our own cruisers could not keep pace. I can recall the HMS *Shropshire* valiantly trying to keep speed with the *Elizabeth* in the Irish Sea. Our bridge finally flashed a rather sarcastic message: 'Don't you think it's time to go home to Mummy!'

Life on board was certainly in dramatic contrast to what Cunard had planned for their transoceanic shuttle. Captain Ashton-Irvine recalled the limitations of such crossings:

The troops were never permitted on deck during my voyages [1942]. Soon after we passed The Narrows in New York harbour, they were sent below and then only to reappear five or six days later, just after we passed the Clyde lighthouse in Scotland. Only the gunners were permitted on deck. Understandably, should the upper decks be littered with humanity during an attack, the gunners simply could not reach their stations. We would have been lost. Many of the troops on those early Atlantic voyages never saw daylight after New York until Scotland. Only on rare occasions were the blacked-out portholes even opened for ventilation.

On board, there was a strong division between Cunard officers, the ship's operational staff and the soldier-passengers. I can only recall visiting the troop quarters twice. There was simply no need for mixing. Furthermore, it was actually quite overwhelming, so incredibly crowded. The only Cunard officers that regularly passed into the troop sections were the two deck officers, who acted as liaisons to the military.

In his memoirs, Commodore Sir James Bisset also describes life aboard the Queens (in his case, specifically the *Mary*) with as many as 16,000 soldier-passengers:

Only two meals a day were served, each of six sittings. Breakfasts were from 6.30am to 11am and dinners from 3pm to 7.30pm.

The officers' dining room — which in peacetime was the tourist-class lounge — seated 350. The troops' mess hall — which was the three-deck-high first-class restaurant — seated 2,000. The mess tables — of metal, with wooden benches — seated an average of eighteen men, with two orderlies to each table. The orderlies formed queues to the kitchens, drew the food in large metal containers, then carried it into the mess hall and dished it out to the tables.

Every sitting lasted forty-five minutes. Every soldier carried his own knife, fork, plate and spoon. The men entered the mess hall at one end, and left it at the other end, to avoid clashing with the queue waiting for the next sitting. The utensils, known as 'eating irons,' were well designed to be hooked together and held on a wire handle. Each man, on filing out of the mess hall, swizzled his gear in a battery of four tanks in succession holding soapy water, boiling fresh water, boiling disinfectant and finally boiling sea-water, and then took it to his quarters to drain dry.

When the *Queen Mary* finally reached Gourock on 7 August 1942, she had survived one of those wartime near-escapes. As she zig-zagged her way some 200 miles north-west of Ireland, a huge explosion occurred quite near to the ship. Water rose 300 ft into the air. The liner rattled in reaction. The vibrations of such a large, speeding vessel had obviously set off an acoustic mine. Had she not been constantly altering her course, she might well have passed directly over the sinister mine. Although she was equipped with thirty lifeboats for 3,000 and enough liferafts for 17,000, abandoning a ship as big and as crowded as the *Mary* under emergency conditions was a prospect to be dreaded.

A month later, in September 1942, both Queens were together at New York, awaiting fresh loads of American troops. At Pier 90, the *Elizabeth* waited for three weeks; the *Mary* for twelve days. The latter left New York on 27 September, to begin a voyage scarred by tragedy, the only serious blemish to the otherwise superb wartime record of the Queens.

On 2 October, once again off north-west Ireland, the *Queen Mary* was met by the cruiser HMS *Curacoa* and four Royal Navy destroyers that were to escort her for the remaining day's run to the Clyde. Both the Cunarder and the *Curacoa* were sailing at top speeds, both in predetermined zigzag fashion. However, at times, the small warship came so close to the liner's bow that the officers on the bridge actually lost sight of her beneath the *Mary*'s vast foredecks. Supposedly, the master of the cruiser miscalculated — by mere seconds — and the *Mary* plunged into her broadside, 'like a knife through butter' as has been so often described. The 3-in armour plating of the smaller vessel was cut through, with each half of the *Curacoa* suddenly drifting along each side of the 81,000-ton *Mary* and then rapidly disappearing in the liner's wake. Although liferafts and rings were tossed from the moving *Queen*, some 338 sailors perished. Only seventy-two survived, rescued by the four other destroyer escorts. As always, the *Mary* was under emphatic orders never to stop, not even in an instance such as this. A U-boat might easily be lurking about and a slowed or, worse still, stopped troopship presented the perfect target. Furthermore, as was later suggested, the cruiser might have exploded upon impact with the liner, resulting in a massive fire and possible destruction of both vessels. The *Mary*'s speed was reduced to 15 knots and emergency repairs to her dented bow, using tons of concrete, were made at Gourock by crews from the John Brown yards. The bow, an almost razor-like creation that was also specially strengthened to meet the possibility of collision and even icebergs, suffered a deep cut. With no dry dock space available in Britain, full repairs had to be made in America. The *Mary* was rerouted to Boston on her next crossing and then, for the second time in her career, entered that port's naval dry dock, from 14 October until 2 November. She then went to New York, where she lay idle for another month, awaiting another load of troops. She finally resumed sailings on 8 December, leaving New York with 10,389 GIs aboard.

Phillip Levin of Merrick, New York was a sergeant major aboard the *Mary* during the tragic collision crossing:

October 2nd was a superbly clear day. We could just about see the Irish coast. I can recount that at 2.07 in the afternoon the lookout raised alarm that a suspected U-boat was spotted on the port bow ahead. In response, the *Mary* wheeled to starboard. In the meanwhile, the *Curacoa* was answering the submarine alert and sped to port. She cut in front of the liner's bow and, because of a split-second miscalculation, was trampled by the larger vessel. I was in the office on the main deck at the time and felt only the slightest rattle and vibration. Actually, it seemed quite normal. But word of the collision spread quickly, like wildfire throughout the ship. I raced to the open, upper decks and looked aft to see the two halves of the *Curacoa* drifting in our wake and then rather quickly sinking. I could see the drowning sailors and also the pick-up of the survivors by the other escort ships, which had raced to the scene. The *Mary* simply continued, uninterrupted and at relatively high speed. We were 20 miles west of Bloody Foreland in Ireland. Word was that if the *Mary*'s damages had penetrated another two feet, some $2 million in gold bullion would have been lost. The valued cargo was in a forward compartment and was being delivered to General Mark Clark and was then to be paid to the French forces in Morocco. When we reached Gourock, concrete was poured into the great dent in the *Queen Mary*'s bow.

Mr W. A. Masson of Aberdeen was also aboard the *Mary* on that fateful crossing. His diary entry for Friday 2 October 1942 reads as follows:

Much better weather today, but still a cold wind blowing. During the night and forenoon, we were rolling quite a bit — there was a swell. Just before luncheon, we were joined by an AA cruiser and six escort vessels [destroyers and corvettes]. The cruiser [the *Curacoa*] took station ahead of us and zig-zagged from one side to the other. At 2.10pm, when passing from starboard to port, we rammed and sank her. She sank in less than ten minutes! Geordie Reed and I were just leaving the weather deck, when we felt the bump (which incidentally was surprisingly slight). We rushed out on deck, and I was just in time to see the cruiser's quarter deck and after turret passing down our starboard side. It was covered in oil and there was no one to be seen. I rushed aft and saw both parts of the cruiser, her stern sticking up, looking for all the world like the *Indefatigable* at Jutland! The forepart of the ship was a distance to the right. The cruiser had been rammed just aft of the after funnel. It was covered in a heavy pall of smoke and steam, then slowly it sank by the bows, then it reared its bow perpendicular — and with a little water foaming round her, she quickly sank. I did not notice what happened to the after part of the cruiser. Soon after, two of the escorts went racing towards the scene. We did not slacken speed at the time of the accident, but later on we cut down to about 15 knots. I did not know the extent of the damage done to our bows. At 4.30pm, land was sighted — the coast of Northern Ireland — at last, home!!!

Mr Norman Blundell, a survivor from the *Curacoa*, kept notes of his experience:

Had the forenoon watch and after eating, went out on to the foc'sle. Just arrived at the top of the ladder by the PO's Heads when the wave hit me — waist high and knocked me over. Looked astern (racing that way) through the bulkhead door, which was open, and saw the stern of a ship sticking up out of the water. (Thought at the time that this must be about a mile away, but since living in Portsmouth and looking at the Isle of Wight over the years, I now consider it must have been 2 or 3 miles away.) Then looked down and realised that it was the stern of our ship, which now had nothing abaft B gun. Very frightened.

The idle *Elizabeth* under guard at New York's Pier 90 in October 1940. She eventually left New York on 13 November to take up trooping duties (*Frank O. Braynard Collection*)

The *Queen Mary* anchored off Cape Town early in the war (*Frank O. Braynard Collection*)

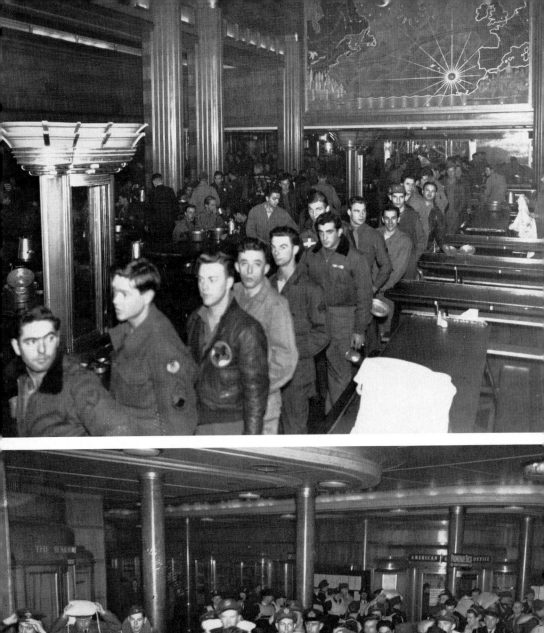

We were listing to starboard at about 30–40°. Clambered (too steep to walk) up the port side of the foc'sle and stood by the guardrail for perhaps thirty seconds and remember:

(a) Jimmy (First Lieutenant to Lt. Cdr. A. Y. Spearman) trying to get people off ship (always wondered what his second name was). No way he was going to get off — should have got a medal.

(b) Clubs (PTI) doing the same thing — another hero — he got off I think. This was port side amidships.

(c) One float-a-net spinning just off port side and, as some tried to get on it, it dragged others under — what bloody stupid things!

(d) The skipper climbing down the side of the bridge, shouting 'Abandon ship'. Bit late by then, but I was all for it.

(e) The ship was listing more this time and I couldn't jump out far enough to miss the side. Some were sliding down and getting caught by the armour belt — nasty!

(f) Blew up my life belt and clambered down to the lower boom, which was sticking out. Don't remember reaching it. I must have been washed off by the swell — very lucky — well clear of the ship. Swam like hell away and, by the time I took a breather and looked back, she had gone and the fuel oil was bubbling up to the surface.

Once in the drink, so far so good. (Having read the subsequent reports that said the *Curacoa* went down in five minutes, I would say that must be about right, but it seemed longer.) I expected more drag when she went down — but never felt I'd be pulled under. Don't remember any noise apart from the shouting. A few of the swimmers seemed to stick their arms up and just go under. Bloody stupid, at least try!

They were also still having trouble with that idiotic float-a-net. Must have been forty or fifty blokes trying to get on and the thing spinning like a top.

I began to think I could be lucky if the destroyers started picking up survivors soon — probably after about three-quarters of an hour. (We subsequently found out that they were some miles ahead doing an ASDIC sweep.)

Spotted something floating about twenty yards (I suppose) away and

Servicemen prepare for dinner in the Main Restaurant aboard the *Mary*. Notice the large map of the North Atlantic in the background. The hands of the clock have been removed as has the lighted crystal that in peacetime represented the ship's movements between Nantucket and Bishop's Rock (*Imperial War Museum*)

A group of soldiers and civilian passengers muster in the *Queen Mary*'s shopping foyer for an emergency drill (*Imperial War Museum*)

swam to it. It was a seat out of a motor boat or cutter. Lucky again. Probably one or one-and-a-half hours after. Laid across it with legs dangling. Pretty comfortable. Shortly after this I realised that there was nobody very close — frightening again and getting cold. Fuel oil splashing over my face and arms. Tasted it for months afterwards and can still remember the taste.

Heavy swell. One minute I could see a long way, the next like being in a pit. Seasick, always was anyway, every trip.

Chaps being picked some distance away — probably those who learned to ride that bloody float-a-net, quite a close bunch together. Should be my turn soon. I've made it! Then destroyer [Hunt Class destroyer HMS *Bramham*] went further away — nobody very close. I became very frightened and started shouting. Still felt okay, but cold and couldn't feel my legs at all. Then, a voice through a megaphone, well-spoken, an officer, something like 'Hang on, we can see you'.

I felt great as a bloke on the quarter deck threw a heaving line, which landed quite close. Megaphone voice shouted, 'Wait, don't leave go' — or something like that — then 'I can get closer'. Then, they backed this great destroyer just like parking a car and the second throw landed across the seat.

My legs wouldn't work and couldn't climb the scramble net. A big chap, Irish, came down and must have carried me up under his arm. Collapsed in a heap on the upper and a tot of neaters [neat rum]. Only out a few seconds and then felt marvellous.

Later, on the main mess deck — shaking hands with chaps I knew and some I didn't, I expect. Tug Wilson was there, I was glad — a smashing chap.

Survival gear a bit small, but who cares. (Sort of auction later of the skipper's chest, which was recovered, and got back my money belt, which I knew had seven two-shilling pieces in it — now oil stained.) PO's mess provided a smashing meal of bacon, beans and tomatoes — plenty of cigarettes and a game of crib — living again. Picked up about 5.30, I think — one of the last I was told.

Later, on the upper deck, passing through Loch Foyle, chatting to a signalman. Aldis flashing to and from the ship/shore. We were doing about 15–20 knots and it seems we were being told there was a speed limit through the Loch, which we were exceeding. The destroyer skipper was apparently ignoring it because he had survivors on board and said no. Felt important.

Once ashore, I had a hot shower at 'Derry [Londonderry] and fuel oil pouring down the drain. Dining room laid out for a meal and what a meal — tables for four with twenty Players by each plate. How did they manage it? Must have been nearly midnight. Plenty of ladies serving. Wonderful! Kept thinking of blokes I knew who weren't there. Basil Iverson, Bob

Abbot from East Grinstead (went to see his mother subsequently).

Captain called everybody together next morning. Seventy-two picked up (God, there were over four hundred on board!) and two had died on the way back or during the night. Must have used up all my luck. He told us to keep our mouths shut.

Don't remember leaving Londonderry on the Sunday morning [4 October], but do remember being given a packed lunch at Glasgow Central before catching the London train.

Mr Blundell spent 4 October 1982 at Dunoon on the Clyde, forty years later: 'A short wallow in nostalgia. Both my wife and I felt quite depressed for a few hours, but thankful too. She didn't quite know me at the time, but we were married in March 1945, two months before the story broke officially as they say.'

The details of the collision were not officially released during the war. However, the Germans somehow got hold of the story and gloated as they reported the incident over Berlin Radio. It was not until May 1945 that the Admiralty even officially acknowledged the loss of the *Curacoa*. Although the Court of Inquiry on this disaster was not finally resolved until 1949 and the *Queen Mary* was thought to be blameless, Cunard was forced to pay a considerable amount in compensation, assuredly far more than the Admiralty itself.

The 800–900 crewmembers aboard the Queens during the war were still managed and employed by Cunard, through its Liverpool headquarters, but were under the full supervision of the Admiralty. Overall, some 10,000 sea-going staff for Cunard ships had to be rotated, relieved and transferred between vessels that often changed routes and then arrived and sailed in high secrecy. The Queens, as the most valuable, were never left unattended, not even when they were at anchor between troop voyages. At Gourock, there was always the possibility of a sudden air attack and thus the need for a very quick get-away.

Two days before Christmas 1942, the *Mary* set sail — on yet another diversion from the North Atlantic — for Suez via Freetown, Cape Town and Aden. She carried 10,669 troops, which included 160 women. Donald A. R. Reynolds of Portsmouth was aboard on that voyage from Gourock to Suez in late 1942:

We sailed from Scotland just two days before Christmas and at our ports of call none of the troops were allowed ashore. I disembarked at Port Tewfik, at Suez. The *Mary* had just been ferrying American GIs across the North Atlantic and was therefore stocked with such luxuries as milk chocolate, which had not been tasted for a long, long time in Britain.

My own 'berth' for the voyage consisted of three 'biscuits' (they were 2 ft square and filled with kapok) laid straight on the promenade deck. The 2ft between me and my neighbour was just about enough for kit-bag, haver-sack, belt, rifle and temporarily discarded clothing. The 'promenading' width was reduced to about 10 ft because there was a row of such 'berths' on the side nearest the sea and two rows of end-to-end 'berths' on the side nearest the so-called 'public rooms' which were used almost exclusively eighteen hours a day for 'Housey Housey' (bingo in post-war language), which is a decidedly monotonous activity to listen to if you are not actually taking part.

The special treat for Christmas dinner was boiled pork followed by sago pudding and, bearing in mind the surfeit of milk chocolate, I leave you to imagine the effect of such a crowded ship two days out into the Atlantic. It is, of course, only hearsay but I always understood the *Mary* went halfway across to the USA before turning south for the long haul around the Cape. But once we got over our initial troubles, it was really quite a pleasant voyage and we felt we had the advantage over other troops who travelled by convoy much more dangerously and slowly. I believe we reached Port Tewfik in twenty-three days.

Once at Suez, the *Mary* was ordered to assist in the movement of 31,400 Australian troops from the Middle East to fortify the defences of their homeland. Four other troopers would also be used: Cunard's *Aquitania*; French Line's *Île de France*, still under P & O wartime management; Holland–America's *Nieuw Amsterdam*; and Furness Withy's *Queen of Bermuda*.

One immediate difficulty was that, as a convoy, the group could only sail at a maximum of 18 knots, the best possible speed of the Furness liner, the smallest vessel in the group. The *Mary* loaded her troop-passengers at Suez and then sailed, on 25 January 1943, for Massawa, where she waited for the *Aquitania* and *Île de France*. Then, the three were ordered to meet with the *Nieuw Amsterdam* and *Queen of Bermuda* in the Gulf of Aden, off Perim. In the final count-ing, the five troopers were loaded as follows:

	Troops	Crew
Queen Mary	9,995	877
Aquitania	6,953	606
Île de France	6,531	675
Nieuw Amsterdam	6,241	465
Queen of Bermuda	1,731	253

Aboard 229,500 tons of valuable wartime ships were 34,327 souls. The *Mary* steamed in the middle with two of the other troopers along each side. A water and refuelling spot was arranged in the Maldive Islands, at Addu Atoll, a remote anchorage some 600 miles southwest of Colombo on Ceylon. The *Mary* reached Sydney on 27 February and remained there for nearly a month, until her departure for home waters in March. Her visit was the last by either of the Queens to Australia. Calling at Cape Town and Freetown en route to Gourock, she carried 8,326 passengers — including 4,050 Italian prisoners, who were being moved from South Africa to Britain for work projects, and also British, French, Dutch, Polish, Norwegian and New Zealand passengers of all types and ranks.

For her next assignment, the *Mary* was to go back on the Atlantic troop shuttle, the preliminary for the projected Allied invasion of Europe. To take up this new assignment, rejoining the *Queen Elizabeth*, the *Mary* proceeded to New York on 5 May, taking 6,235 passengers, which included 4,350 German prisoners-of-war, who were being cleared out of British camps and sent to America for further internment. Once at New York, these prisoners were offloaded into tenders in the Lower Bay before the liner continued to Pier 90.

Prior to resuming Atlantic service, the *Mary* was dry-docked for six days, for the first time in the confines of New York harbour. She went to the new 1,080ft-long graving dock at Bayonne, New Jersey, just south of the Statue of Liberty. Over a dozen tugs carefully manoeuvred the liner into the US Navy facility. The only other dry docks on the American side for the Queens were at Boston and Newport News, Virginia. Several other facilities, with sufficient dock space, had various drawbacks such as bridge clearances or depth problems. Over three decades later, the *Mary*'s successor, *Queen Elizabeth 2*, would use the same Bayonne graving dock on several occasions.

The *Queen Mary* was to make a continuous series of transatlantic troop voyages between New York and Gourock, from 1 June 1943 until 26 August 1944. Only then did she make a detour for one round voyage to Halifax. During this period, she was dry-docked once more, for five days in September 1943, again at Bayonne. Her next full overhaul and dry dock phase would not come until November 1944. Also during these years, the *Elizabeth* used the Bayonne facility.

The Queens seemed miraculously free from attack. With their high speeds, constant zigzagging and highly secret courses, they became known as 'the grey ghosts'. Generally, they arrived at and sailed from port in a cloak of darkness, with all their lights extinguished. On clear, moonlit nights, they appeared as enormous silhouettes, gliding past the horizon at a rapid pace. Sometimes, at sea, the Queens were detoured as far north as Iceland; at other times, south to the Azores. Their ever-changing courses were determined mostly from Whitehall, being plotted on large-scale maps of the North Atlantic with tiny wooden ship models. The models were constantly moved in reaction to the latest intelligence reports of German 'wolf packs' of submarines. If reports of danger were received, special coded messages were sent to the Queens to alter course. The signal code books used on board were changed almost constantly. Familiarisation and even memorisation was therefore no simple feat for the radio operators. The Queens would also be given reports on icebergs, sinkings, possible derelicts and the courses of convoys as well as independent ships. Rarely were the heavily loaded *Mary* and *Elizabeth* seen in the North Atlantic by other ships during the war years.

In November 1942, Berlin Radio did report that a U-boat had damaged the *Elizabeth*. Supposedly, she was hit on 9 November, some 200 miles north-west of Ireland, while bound for New York with over 7,300 passengers who were mostly evacuees from Britain.

Horst Kessler was then the commanding officer of U-704.

We were west of Ireland, headed for the Bay of Biscay. The weather was quite bad: a Force 8 blowing, snow gusts and visibility constantly changing. The bridge watch was belted to the tower and we could not use binoculars because of constantly overcoming seas.

We were returning to base [at La Pallice in France], primarily because we were low on fuel, but also because we were damaged in an Allied air raid the day before. The Junkers compressor had been torn away and the forward torpedo tubes were leaking seawater. Overall, however, we were safe and could be repaired, the crew was well and we had five electric torpedoes left, one in each of the four forward tubes and one in the stern tube.

At about 1pm, on the 9th, the bridge watch called to report a big ship at 30° to port. The big steamer could be made out with the naked eye: two huge funnels, two masts and, when our boat crested a wave, we could see parts of the vessel's bridge. Our position in relation to the steamer was 6–7 miles. I ordered 'all men to battle stations, dive to periscope depth, tube 1 through 4 for underwater firing.

While these preparations were being made, I checked the Weyher reference book to try to identify the steamer. Within a few minutes, our chief engineer brought the sub to periscope depth. I was able to make out the steamer's deck. I believe she must have been the *Queen Elizabeth*.

The forward tubes were made ready and the preangle calculator [an aiming device] was adjusted according to calculated data: target's position was 70° to the right, speed 28 knots. This resulted in a preangle of 52°, aiming breadth 300 metres, a fan of four torpedoes to be fired at a range of 2,000 metres.

I ordered 'muzzle caps' [torpedo tube doors] to be opened. Meanwhile, our boat was turned on to an attack course diagonal to the target's course, and both our engines put at half-ahead. I was at the periscope, turning it in the direction in which the *Queen Elizabeth*'s propeller noises indicated she would appear. Then, within nine minutes of our first sighting of the steamer, all ready — we were at periscope depth and making 'both slow'. [While submerged, U-boats ran on electric motors.] Both motors were now at 'slow ahead', despite the heavy seas. We made a slight adjustment to the fire-bearing and then fired the fan of torpedoes just as the periscope cut under the waves. We then dove to 20 metres to wait, our eyes hanging on the stop-watch, to listen to the detonation. This followed after scarcely two minutes. [Kessler referred only to a single detonation. The other three torpedoes either passed beneath the liner or missed completely because of the heavy seas.] Soon afterward, our sound men reported that the steamer had stopped.

We still had one torpedo, the one in the stern tube. We realised that the ship was no more than 2,000–3,000 metres away. I ordered the boat to the periscope depth. However, there were dense snow gusts and visibility was under 100 metres. We proceeded under water with both engines 'full ahead', following the torpedo track toward the big steamer. The visibility was bound to improve and, since the target had stopped, she could hardly escape.

Five minutes later, with the visibility still very poor, we returned to periscope depth. Our sound man reported that the steamer's propellers were again turning, making very high revolutions as before. She had escaped. That one hit, the sound we heard, had obviously not damaged the steamer's engines. I felt that perhaps another U-boat was nearby and would try to hit her.

To this day, the complete authenticity of this incident as told by Horst Kessler is in question. Kessler, who lives in West Germany, still maintains that it is true. In 1947, at the British War Court hearings in Hamburg, most British naval personnel present scoffed at the idea. However, one officer persisted and later found, in the Cunard records, that the *Elizabeth*'s bridge officers recorded a 'heavy detonation' at 1pm on 9 November 1942. The liner was stopped for fifteen minutes (a serious violation of the wartime rules for the Queens) but then restarted her engines and moved on.

Berlin Radio reported the day after the incident that the battleship HMS *Queen Elizabeth* had been hit. Kessler radioed Berlin to clarify that he had attacked the liner and not the battleship. There was the suggestion that the Nazi High Command made the mistake deliberately. Several weeks later, in a speech in the House of Commons, Winston Churchill called the attack 'an outright lie'. The British Government maintains still that no such attack ever took place. Unfortunately, certain records for that particular period in the *Elizabeth*'s career have now simply disappeared.

Supplying the Queens was another enormous production, a magnificent effort in itself. Both liners had priority status and were therefore loaded with all essentials, even despite the many shortages caused by the war. Alone, the *Mary* burned off 1,000 tons of fuel every twenty-four hours. Although most sailings to Gourock took five days, she usually sailed with 8,000 tons of fuel on board, a serious precaution should any extensive changes be made in her routing. She also carried 6,500 tons of fresh water, which was consumed at the rate of 700–800 tons per day. The drinking water was always chlorinated and filtered. Seawater was used in the bathrooms, for toilets, washing decks and every other possible way where fresh water could be conserved.

The *Mary*, like the *Elizabeth*, was loaned to the US Government during the war, but remained a British flagship, still owned by Cunard, but under final orders from the Admiralty in London. The ships were considered part of the 'Reverse Lend-Lease'. However, to the many hundreds of thousands of American servicemen who crossed in the liners, the *Mary* and *Elizabeth* were and only could be American ships: 'After all, who else could build such mighty vessels!'

The operating staff for the Queens numbered between 800–900 during the war years on the Atlantic. On a troop crossing in June 1943, the *Mary* had a listed complement of 927, which was divided as 120 in the deck department, 258 in the engine department, 430 in the catering department and 119 permanent staff. Their tasks and ratings ranged from the carpenters and deck boys to police and fire officers, to staff captains and the Cunard commodore himself.

Captain Eric Ashton-Irvine recalled:

To Cunard staff members, the wartime Queens were actually unpopular assignments. They ran a rushed and often frightening service on the Atlantic, the shore leaves were infrequent and the conditions in general rather harsh. As a junior officer, my own quarters on the *Elizabeth* were incredibly tiny and spartan. The officers' accommodation had never been fully fitted out in 1940 and so we made do with second-hand furniture from the shipyard and bare steel walls and overheads. We slept in these 'matchboxes' and socialised in an equally cramped officers' mess. I recall climbing over the coffee tables just to reach the exit.

To the general staff, the working conditions — even in that wartime period — were quite extreme. For example, the kitchen staffs began serving their first meals at six in the morning and their last meals at ten in the evening.

A shopping list for one of the Queens for a five-day voyage with over 15,000 troops and 900 crew was quite staggering:

124,300lb of potatoes
53.600lb of butter, eggs and powdered milk
31,000lb of sugar, tea and coffee
29,000lb of fresh fruit
31,000lb of canned fruit

    18,000lb of jam
     4,600lb of cheese
    155,000lb of meat and poultry
    21,500lb of ham and bacon
    76,000lb of flour and cereals

There were nine canteens aboard the ships, selling soft drinks, cigarettes, and sweets, but absolutely no chewing gum. It had become a troublesome nuisance to the ships' staff, who spent hours scraping it from the decks, bulkheads and handrails. Gum was banned aboard both Queens for the duration of the war.

At their New York berth, at the foot of 50th Street and Twelfth Avenue, the Queens were guarded by a special military police force of 750 men. Every precaution had to be taken. Rumour of sabotage was frequent. However, even with their special protection, the fire hoses on the *Elizabeth* were once found to be plugged deliberately with bottle caps and on another occasion, during a drill, several lifeboats began to sink when lowered in the Hudson. It was later discovered that tiny holes had been drilled in each of the boats. In April 1943, several bombs were found under a pile of blankets aboard the *Elizabeth*. Upon discovery, they were immediately tossed overboard, into the murky waters of the Hudson. It was never known whether or not they were real or merely dummies. Rather strangely, a subsequent brief investigation did hint that the bombs were probably of British origin. The importance of security at the time is perhaps best illustrated by a 'pep talk' delivered by the commander of the military police at Pier 90, while guarding the *Queen Mary*. He said, 'You begin to guard a ship so vital to the United Nations that if it meant choosing between your safety and that of that vessel, I would necessarily sacrifice every man in the company.'

Embarkation for the Queens, meaning an orderly and systematic boarding of over 15,000 service personnel, who had most likely never even been aboard a ship, usually meant a major conference about three days before sailing. This process occurred week after week, for well over two years. Sizeable parties of advance teams — including officers, military police and special guides, and usually numbering between 2,000 and 2,500 — would meet, then tour the ships for familiarisation. The quarters would then be divided into red, white and blue areas. Forward, from the bow aft to the main stairway and excluding the sun deck above was the 'red area'. Midships, from the main stairway aft to the former cabin-class smoking room and including the sun deck above was the 'white area'. Aft, from the cabin-class smoking room to the very stern of the ship was the 'blue area'.

Many troops scheduled for embarkation on either the *Mary* or *Elizabeth* received special training at Camp Kilmer, across the Hudson in New Jersey. Enormous wooden mock-ups of the two Queens had been created, including gangways, as the troops practised the boarding process. Each operation was filmed and then shown in the camp theatre to point out mistakes and improvements. The result was that almost everyone knew how to board and where to go once on board the ships. Every detail was considered. The soldiers were even made familiar with places to store their kit-bags and where they would sleep and eat. Almost every embarkation session was therefore efficiently completed within twelve hours.

The troops would arrive the night before sailing, either aboard ferries, which would be berthed at the outer end of Pier 90, or on buses, which came alongside on Twelfth Avenue. Beginning at about 7pm and continuing until about 1am, the troops would march on board. Each would be given an assignment card or a coded metal disc, in one of the three appropriate colours, showing where he would sleep, eat and muster for emergency drills. Once settled in, it would be 'lights out' until 6am. The next morning, just prior to sailing, there would be a series of musters and instruction sessions outlining the ship's routine, the emergency drills, black-outs, air-raid procedures and abandon-ship methods. The air-raid drill, usually held before the ship left the confines of the Hudson River, ordered every man to take cover in the lower-deck sleeping quarters. Alternately, the emergency drills had everyone mustering on the upper, open-air decks. These drills were repeated throughout the voyage and, on occasion, at night so that the troops would become familiar with darkened conditions. Immediate instruction was given on the proper application of a lifejacket. Strict orders were that every man should carry his lifejacket at all times. The penalty for failure to do so was to surrender one's shoes, sometimes one at a time, for a pre-scribed period. The only men excepted from these near-constant drills were the gun crews, submarine lookouts, mess orderlies, kitchen assistants and 'the sweeping parties'. These latter members of the ships' staff had the almost never-ending chore of keeping the troopers free of litter. Wartime passengers, be they military or civilian, were subject also to prohibitions against personal radio sets, electric razors, travel irons, flashlights, knives useable as weapons, cameras, obscene language and heavy gambling. Smoking was not permitted on deck at night nor in the troop cabins and compartments or along the ships' corridors.

Captain Ashton-Irvine recalled another prohibition and sub-sequent penalty for crossing one of the three colour sections: 'If a GI assigned to the blue section of the ship were to cross into the red section, which was often nothing more than a painted stripe, he might be "grabbed" by one of the MPs [military police] and given a special assignment. These were mostly in the form of extra duty, assisting the Cunard staff with general chores and maintenance.'

For diversion and entertainment during the five-day troop cros-sings, there were often two film showings a day as well as periodic concerts, often of a questionable quality. The ships were supplied also with portable record players and records, games, puzzles and playing cards. Religious services were offered as well.

Mr J. Currie of Southsea crossed on the Queens during the war in 1943:

We left from Gourock in mid-February. Being Royal Navy, I was allotted a watch on a twin Bofors gun, eight hours off and four on. Everything outside at night was pitch darkness, no lights whatsoever. If you opened the door to go on deck, all the lights automatically went out in that area. Consequently, it wasn't very nice going to the guns at midnight as it was often rough, the ship rolling madly and pitch dark. You inched your way along the deck to get to the ladder that led to the bridge. You never knew the minute you were going to be either washed or blown overboard. Once, I stood watch for four hours with soaking-wet feet. As we steamed to New York, we zigzagged all the way. The armament, I believe, was Pom Poms, Bofors guns, and, I believe, a 6-in gun on the stern. The *Queen* had her own wartime gunners, but we were stand-by in case anyone was hurt. The ship had action stations, move about the decks. I was lying on my bunk at one point, watching an oilskin swinging on the door and trying to calculate the number of degrees, which to my mind was not far off forty-five.

The nicest view was pulling into New York, from a distance. The Statue of Liberty. The skyscrapers. The band playing to greet us and the ship's hooters going. We pulled into Pier 90, greeted by the Red Cross as we had some wounded on board. I was given cigarettes and a sewing kit. I watched a young man give an exhibition of baton twirling, at a concert on board. He was wearing an RAF uniform. It was Hughie Green, then a young man. Seems like yesterday.

I was going to Bermuda to meet a carrier, but it sailed before I could make it. I had a spell in New York instead and was made to feel most welcome. We used to go the Union Jack Club and get free passes for the shows and dances. I managed to go to the 'Stage Door Canteen' and even had a bit of roller-skating on a rink in New York City. I was taken to the Bronx and Brooklyn and met quite a lot of people over there. I also managed to see an uncle and cousin of mine over the river [in New Jersey]. I remember some big liner [the *Normandie*] lying on its side. Think it had been gutted by fire. I was based at Pier 90, in a big warehouse converted into a barracks on the dockside about the bottom of Fiftieth Street. I spent about two and a half months there. Never got to bed until three in the morning any night. It was quite an experience.

I was ordered to the docks one midnight to join the *Queen Elizabeth*, sailing for Gourock. This time, I was given the job of watch-keeper on the bridge. Same voyage procedures coming home, but I didn't quite like finding my way to the bridge in the dark. Another very rough sea, resulting in more wet feet as the waves were coming over the decks. Same zigzagging pattern. No trouble, but anyone falling overboard was lost. There was no stopping allowed. It was too risky. It was very difficult to use the toilets as there was always much seasickness. Some of us would go inside one of the funnels to keep warm as it was very cold and windy. We arrived at Gourock after six days and got the train to Glasgow.

Mr Denis Money of Portsmouth sailed in the *Elizabeth* in December 1943:

My first contact with the *Queen Elizabeth* was coming alongside her in Gourock waters, disembarking from the dwarfed paddle steamer and entering her by the bowels, so to speak, through a gaping aperture in the port side.

This was approaching Christmas 1943 and was the prelude to one of the most hazardous outward-bound voyages of the *Elizabeth*, when she was caught by the most virulent storms ever experienced by that intrepid war-time trooper. The sea was extremely turbulent and much to the chagrin of the galley staff, very few of the Forces — only some 500 odd — were able to participate in the superb Christmas lunch that was served. I remember being pressed to accept gargantuan portions of Christmas fare, being one of the fortunates to escape the *mal de mer*.

One of the most bizarre experiences still vivid in my mind was attending the Christmas Eve carol service in what was the first-class lounge — plush even in wartime garb. Those attending were seated in wicker armchairs, the splayed feet of which sank into deep-piled carpet. Midway through the service, the ship suddenly heeled over in excess of 30° and, like some fantasy, all the seated passengers slid towards the bulkhead. Needless to say, the programme continued. Afterwards, we learnt that the sonar had picked up a submarine sounding and the helm of the unescorted *Queen* was flung over — the ship making a 45° change in direction.

The culmination of events occurred when the *Queen Elizabeth* was caught between the crests of some 40ft waves during the night and dropped bodily into the trough, resulting in many injuries, including three fatalities, when those manning the guns on the upper decks plunged to their deaths as the ship plummeted down. Among the most seriously injured were those accommodated in the troop quarters aft in five-tiered bunks. When the ship literally dropped, many of those in the upper bunks crashed down on the deck below. Fortunately, I was housed in one of the adapted first-class cabins and landed with a jolt safely on my bunk. The severity of the accident was clearly visible the next morning. The huge steel stanchions to the fore mast had been torn away together with all the 'Karley floats' attached to them.

After the months of black-out experienced in and around the UK it was like a fairyland to sail into the tranquil waters past the Statue of Liberty and to see the twinkling lights of the renowned New York skyline.

Mr R. S. Trout of Southampton also experienced a stormy passage aboard the *Mary* on the return crossing after the *Curacoa* collision in October 1942:

I was in the RAF, bound for some flying training in America. It was just after the *Mary* had rammed and sunk HMS *Curacoa*. When we boarded her at anchorage at Gourock, her bow had been filled with concrete and the anchor cable flanked around her broken stem for additional support. We sailed to Boston, where she was to be dry-docked for permanent repairs. Despite the damages, we crossed unaccompanied and at high speed.

What I particularly remember is the storm we encountered on the way over. I was one of a party of four airmen under a sergeant whose daily fatigue was to wash down all the flights of a staircase way up forward. With the ship pitching badly, this duty was a most unexpected problem. When the bow was rising (like some high-speed lift), you couldn't get the mop out of the bucket. It was as if it was nailed down. When the bow was falling, mop and bucket were determined to get airborne and you had to hang on tightly to the handrail to avoid doing the same. Any mopping activity had to be carried out in the brief seconds when the bow was stationary between rise and fall. Eventually, the sergeant and the three others were prostrate with seasickness. I became a working party of one. Then, I slipped on the wet stairs and ended up on the next deck down with mop and upturned bucket beside me. I decided that the RAF didn't want me to start my flying career with a broken leg and so returned the gear to store and stayed away until a recovered sergeant came looking for me!

Mr Ralph L. Carver, now of Cherry Hill, New Jersey, crossed aboard the *Elizabeth* in 1944:

I was a Heavy Weapons Platoon Sergeant, in Company D, 1st Battalion, 345th Infantry Regiment, 87th Division. We came from Fort Jackson, South Carolina to Fort Kilmer in New Jersey. Later, we crossed the Hudson by ferry and what a sight the *Elizabeth* was, even in war dress!

We were among the first troops to board her that day. The knowledge that we would be shipping out on the *Queen* helped set my mind at ease and I'm sure others understood the significance of crossing the Atlantic in a fast ship rather than a slow convoy. We were assigned to one of the duty battalions and it was our task to assist the Cunard crew during the voyage. Of course, the ship was divided into three sections: forward, mid and aft. A duty battalion was assigned to each section. Furthermore, each section had their colour: red, white and blue. We were in the forward red section. It was absolutely mandatory that all troops remained in the section in which they bunked. You could not venture from section to section without proper authority. Most of the troops did, in fact, remain in their section.

That first evening on board was a lonely and reflective time. The main body of troops would arrive the following day. From deck, the New York City skyline looked magnificent. We would have given anything to get a pass into town. Just one last time, but it was not to be. Would we ever see it again? We wondered and perhaps prayed a bit.

We wandered through our part of the *Elizabeth*, deck by deck and marvelled at its size and luxury. Even stripped as she was for troop service, her grandeur was still evident. If you closed your eyes, you could imagine how she would be in peacetime — the luxury, the music, laughter and fun. Who would have thought that a poor kid from north-western Pennsylvania would be sailing in one of the fabulous Queens, even in wartime?

Being a duty officer on the *Elizabeth* turned out to be a great plus. We were not required to attend any drills or troop formations. We were also given permanent berths for the entire voyage. We were six or eight men to a small stateroom on C deck. Alternately, the troops on the upper decks had to rotate nightly. One night, they would sleep on deck, which although sheltered could get quite chilly. The other night, they could sleep in one of the large converted staterooms, which could get quite crowded.

One of the biggest benefits in my personal case was the food. I would report with my platoon at the foot of the main stairway in the forward section of the ship. The platoons were then broken up into three or four smaller groups and turned over to a ship's purser or officer. They left for whatever assignments were given to them. One of my jobs was to help move food from the provision lockers to the kitchens. I would finish this assignment by spending time in the kitchens. The kitchen staff were wonderful and we had access to all we wanted to eat — hot bread, butter, jam, coffee or tea. Working the food lockers soon became a problem. Everyone wanted that assignment.

Needless to say, the boys became quite adept at smuggling food out of the lockers. We had boxes of cheese, meat and bread in our room. Whatever was available, we had. We were eating so well that the only time we went to the ship's mess was the first night on board. Guess we had little appreciation for English rations and preparation!

We worked only two or three hours each day. The rest of the time was our own and we had the run of our section. The only exception was that if we were not on duty, we had to stay in our quarters during all drills and/or formations.

We sailed on October 16th [1944]. It was an emotional day for all of us. It seemed that for hours we could continue to see land off the port bow. We were sailing almost parallel to the coast [Long Island]. I loved the sea and could spend hours just enjoying its beauty.

It was not the same with many others, however. Most of the men on board wanted no part of the sea and their reason for remaining on deck was quite simply out of fear. They were afraid of being trapped if we were torpedoed. Many had expected to be sailing in a convoy and felt it would be safer. They

The *Queen Elizabeth*'s forward First Class Observation Bar, stripped of its luxurious amenities and converted as a troop dormitory with standee berths (*Frank O. Braynard Collection*)

The former Cabin Class Gymnasium aboard the *Queen Elizabeth* was converted to sleep over fifty service personnel (*Frank O. Braynard Collection*)

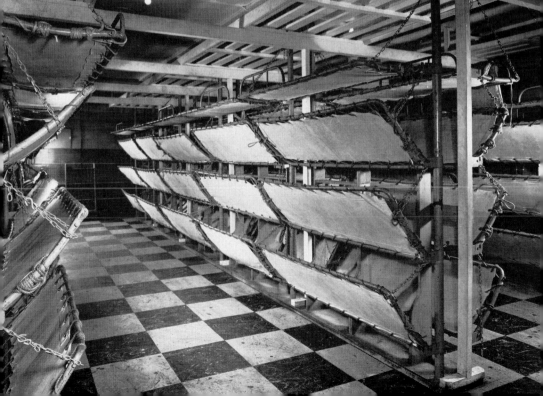

couldn't understand why we were sailing alone and no amount of explaining could convince them that we were far luckier to be on the largest and fastest ship afloat and therefore much safer. An enemy sub would have to be in the right place at the right time or just be very, very lucky to get a shot at us. They couldn't believe that it was actually the large convoys that were really much more dangerous. In addition, we would be at sea less than half the time it would have taken in a slow convoy. We were also much more comfortable, with much better accommodations and much smoother sailing.

This wasn't to say there wasn't any seasickness. There was plenty of it. I can recall standing at the rail with several GIs, one of whom was expressing his fears and then complaining he didn't feel well. Suddenly, he looked kind of funny and then, without warning, upchucked. That day, we all learned that it was not wise to stand at the windward rail with the wind in your face with a companion who didn't feel well.

The card games on board are also vivid in my memory. They started almost as soon as the ship sailed. Myself, I was not a gambler, but was fascinated watching. On the deck below ours was a large indoor swimming pool. It was not in use and covered over for the duration of the war. The space was used as a kind of recreation room. Mostly, it was used for cards: Poker, Blackjack, Craps and, of all things, the Game of Hearts — and often all at the same time. The really big game was Hearts. As kids we played this, but never considered it a serious game of chance. How little I knew! That game started just as we left New York, went on for twenty-four hours a day and did not finally break up until we dropped anchor off Scotland. Many, many dollars were won and lost. The other card games started and stopped. Hearts never did. When one player would drop out, another would take his place.

The voyage lasted five days, but was uneventful. The ship constantly changed course, but one really wasn't aware of this unless you observed the motion and the sea very closely. I don't recall any close calls, but then as one of the troops, we wouldn't have been told except for the very obvious.

We arrived in the Firth of Clyde on the 22nd [October 1944] and dropped anchor off Gourock at 0730 hrs. We had to remain in our quarters, but the crew opened the large doors in the side of the hull. It was from these that we would disembark. Later, I can recall observing the countryside through the

The *Queen Mary*'s indented bow following her collision with HMS *Curacoa* in October 1942. On her next crossing to America, she went to the Boston Navy Yard for full repairs (*Frank O. Braynard Collection*)

Summer sailing: the forward section of the *Queen Mary* during one of her crossings to Gourock (*Imperial War Museum*)

doors and being absolutely tantalised by the beauty of the place and the contrast of this port as compared to the port of New York. It was much like being anchored in the middle of the country on the largest ship in the world. It was a total surprise when we were expecting an industrial port.

More specifically, I remember the very vivid colours. The early morning light, the patches of blue sky and the rays of sunshine coming down through the grey, low-hanging clouds. The clouds cast shadows over the various shades of blue, green and grey of the surrounding hills and waters. There were pretty towns in the distance. It was all like a picture postcard.

We soon left the *Elizabeth* and boarded trains, our destination unknown. My Division ended up in various towns in an area just south of Liverpool, at about 2300 hrs the same day. Two names I remember are Congleton and Stoke-on-Trent. Our Company was billeted in what appeared to be an old factory. This ended our voyage to England.

I will never forget the *Queen* and her wonderful crew. I suppose there were other wartime passengers like myself, who dreamed of sailing on her again in peacetime when she regained her glamour and luxury. Last year [1982], I watched as the *Queen Elizabeth 2* sailed along the Delaware River to Philadelphia and was again reminded, nearly forty years later, of sailing in such a beautiful ship. I suppose that in my heart I was again seeing the original *Elizabeth*.

Mrs Margaret Lewis of Eastbourne has a slightly different recollection of the *Elizabeth*. She sailed westbound in the liner in 1943 as one of only four female Services personnel on board:

I was a serving ATS and was en route to Washington, DC to work with the Joint Staff Mission (Combined Chiefs of Staff). We were the only ATS on board — lost among the thousands of British and American servicemen. Specifically, I remember that there were lots of young RAF men going to Canada for pilot training. As far as I can recall, the only other female on board was a WAAF, who was being repatriated to her home in California. Say no more! The four of us shared two cabins and we had guards posted at night at each end of the passage! I think that I might qualify for some further title as I was badly bitten by bed bugs during the first night out — surely indicating that the fumigation procedure between trips had missed my bunk.

My most lasting memory was the food. The *Queen Elizabeth* was stocked with all sorts of American goodies. Oh, the white rolls, unlimited butter, ice cream, roast meats, etc!!! All too much for our unaccustomed stomachs.

The black-out on board was absolute, of course. All portholes were blacked over and never, ever opened. On the first day out, we three ATS were put in charge of the ship's library. I can vividly remember walking round the deck in daytime and seeing the deck rails literally covered with the carved initials and graffiti of servicemen, who had made earlier trips. Also, I cannot forget the distant view of the occasional iceberg.

Mrs Lewis retained her berthing card and officer's dining-room card which read:

BERTHING CARD	OFFICERS' DINING ROOM
M Deck	'R' Deck Aft
Room No. 17	Table No. 72
(Retain this Card)	Name_____
	Breakfast: 8.30 AM, Luncheon 1.00 PM,
	Dinner 7.00 PM.

Wartime crossings in the Queens were not often tranquil, however. Dr Joseph McGuire, in his published memoirs *The Sea My Surgery*, recounted a particularly nasty wartime passage for the *Elizabeth*, when heavy seas continuously smashed at the great ship:

We suddenly hit a freak wave, a great mountainous mass of green water. The *Elizabeth*'s bow rose skywards and then disappeared down into a vast trough. As she did, another enormous roller came from nowhere and punched her bows even further downwards. We just continued to go down. I was thrown clean out of bed and could not stand upright. 'This is it', I thought, even though I couldn't fully believe it. There was a deafening roar like nothing I have ever heard before. Every plate vibrated as our propellers rose out of the sea and then raced in thin air. For a measureless moment, the ship seemed to stand on her nose. Finally, slowly, so very slowly, she dragged her forepart from the water, and I found I had been holding my breath.

Then the loud-hailers started booming, calling for carpenters and joiners from among the troops we were transporting to New York. Every skilled man was needed — and fast. That colossal sea had punched the ship's foredeck down and out of shape by six inches. The forepeak was flooded. Every forward capstan was out of commission. Both anchors were jammed.

The second vicious sea had also smashed squarely against the bridge, shattered the thick plate-glass windows, washed the quartermaster from the wheel and flung the deck messenger from the wheelhouse to the wing of the bridge. The staff captain, whose cabin was immediately under the bridge, was shaving when the wave struck. A block of plate-glass from his window was stove-in in one piece, ricocheted from a panel, hit him flat and then knocked him down. In two seconds, he was sitting, dazed, waist-deep in water.

When I went up to attend him I talked with another white-faced officer on the bridge. He was suffering from minor shock. His line of vision, he told me, as the *Elizabeth* went down and down towards the bed of the ocean, was from the bridge window through the crow's nest on the foredeck to where the ship's bow should normally have been. The hawse-pipes, like two huge frightened eyes, must have been straight down towards the bottom of the Atlantic.

Mr R. M. Mills of London was also aboard a particularly stormy crossing, but on the *Queen Mary* in 1944:

I never imagined, not even in my wildest fantasies, that such a large, solid-looking ship could roll and roll and roll and then continuously wait before righting herself. It was horrifying. You were never sure if the *Mary* would swing back, but instead heel over and capsize. For five full days, until just hours before reaching Scotland, we heaved and tossed. Everything on board creaked and rattled and loose objects always went crashing to the floors. It was almost impossible to sleep. The ship moaned around the clock. At one point, several exhausted, nerve-tense soldiers near to me on C deck began to scream out in absolute fear and terror. I have never seen such frightened faces, not even in the most dangerous combat. There seemed to be a hope-lessness about our state, captives of the storm- and sea-battered *Queen*. Those soldiers went into mild shock, screaming and even crying, their faces flush white. The doctors were summoned. Only mild sedatives could help. To their final moments on board, they remained convinced that we were going to die aboard a capsized *Queen Mary*.

Years later, in the sixties, it was a badly rolling *Mary* that inspired a book and then a major film entitled *The Poseidon Adventure*, which detailed the capsizing of a major liner during a violent storm.

Fortunately, the Queens were designed and built for the rigours of the cruellest North Atlantic sea. Captain Ashton-Irvine thought them to be exceptionally solid ships: 'If you hit a wall with one of the Queens, the wall suffered. Of course, during the worst storms, we would lose countless windows. I was even aboard the *Elizabeth* in a powerful sea when seven decks were slightly bent out of shape.'

Within the relatively calm waters of New York harbour, the Queens usually sailed in the pre-dawn or early morning hours, and were given naval and air escorts until well out into the open Atlantic.

76

Special precautions had to be taken to prevent crowding on one side of the ship by as many as 15,000 personnel, all of them wanting to bid farewell to the Statue of Liberty or the legendary Manhattan skyline. Sir James Bisset, who as a captain was most often in command of the *Mary* during the war years, wrote in his memoirs:

The underwater section of the Queens is almost box-shaped and flat-bottomed amidships. When the *Mary* listed 10 degrees, her draft on the low side was increased by 4 feet. In the narrow and relatively shallow waters of the Hudson River and Upper New York Bay, she had to be kept on an even trim. Fifteen thousand troops on the upper decks represented an additional 1,000 tons of mobile humanity!

Great care and implicit instructions were given prior to each departure from New York. What delay and embarrassment would occur should one of the Queens run aground in New York harbour or, far worse still, capsize due to overloading! On some sailings, many of the troops were asked to remain below decks, where there was often a mad rush for the few porthole openings.

The Queens even carried a good number of celebrities during the war years. Fred Astaire, Bob Hope, Katherine Cornell, Sir Thomas Beecham, Bing Crosby, Douglas Fairbanks, Mickey Rooney, Alexander Korda and Basil Dean were among the more famous who made wartime crossings. However, the most noted single passenger was unquestionably Winston Churchill.

Churchill travelled to Quebec in August 1943 for a special conference with President Roosevelt. The *Mary* was selected to carry him, because of her high speed and the comfort and security that could be offered to the Prime Minister and his party. Consequently, she was detoured off the New York/Gourock troop shuttle for a special round trip to Halifax. She sailed from Gourock on 5 August, reaching Nova Scotia four days later.

The Churchill party consisted of 150 members — including Mrs Churchill and her youngest daughter, Mary, the First Lord of the Admiralty, Admiral Sir Dudley Pound, Lord Louis Mountbatten, and a small army of guards, typists and secretaries. The entire main deck was reserved and sealed off for the 'secret passengers'. Churchill himself was accommodated in one of the former suites on main deck, which had been thoughtfully refurnished and specially cleaned. Adjacent was a special dining room for fourteen, a conference room and a map room. A special communications room could link Churchill with either side of the Atlantic should the emergency arise. The liner's special wartime 'dry laws' were lifted specifically for the Churchill party.

During this particular voyage, cruisers escorted the *Mary* throughout. Rumour was that Hitler offered a £50,000 reward to the U-boat captain who would sink her. However, the customary high secrecy succeeded. Apart from senior government personnel in London and Washington, few knew the whereabouts of the Prime Minister for those five days. Because the *Mary* rarely, if ever, sent wireless messages during the war, the Prime Minister's endless communications were flashed by Morse lamp to a nearby cruiser, which then darted away for a hundred or so miles and safely transmitted the messages by radio.

Churchill was given a rousing reception at Halifax. The intended secrecy of his arrival turned into a jubilant welcome that included a dockside speech by the great leader himself. The *Mary* then waited at Halifax for eighteen days, intending to return Churchill and his entourage to Britain. Instead, at the last minute, Churchill and his immediate staff returned by Royal Navy cruiser. The remainder of the original party joined 14,989 Canadian troops on the *Mary* for the run to Gourock.

By the end of 1943, the Queens had, in that single, most decisive year of the war, brought 320,500 American and Canadian service personnel to Britain. Their work was calculated to be the equivalent of that of twenty normal-sized troopers.

On Christmas Day 1943, the *Mary* was at sea, between New York and Scotland with 12,077 aboard, when a special holiday message was received from Her Majesty Queen Mary. The dowager Queen, like some national treasure, had been reluctantly moved out of London, in September 1939, to a secret hideaway 'in the country'. Travelling with an entourage of sixty-three servants and their dependants, seventy pieces of luggage and several truckloads of favourite furniture, she became the house-guest of the Duke and Duchess of

Beaufort at Badminton. She remained her regal self at all times; even in flash, night-time air raids, she went to the shelter dressed in diamonds and pearls, her beloved needle-point in hand, to await the 'all clear'.

Queen Mary sent a second message to the liner that bore her name, in July 1944, a month after the 'D Day' invasion of Normandy:

Since I launched the *Queen Mary* nearly ten years ago, almost half of her life has been spent on active war service. Now, as the war enters on this decisive phase, I send my warm greetings to the Captain, his officers and the ship's company, and to all those who sail in the ship that bears my name. It is always a source of pride and pleasure to me to receive news of the magnificent work the *Queen Mary* is doing in the transport of troops from every corner of the Empire and Commonwealth, and from the United States of America, to the theatres of war. I pray that before very long it may be her joyful duty to carry the victorious soldiers of the United Nations back to their homes and families in many parts of the world.

Between February and July of 1944, the *Mary* made six crossings to Britain, delivering 74,504 troops. Westbound to New York, she was now more often carrying civilian and special passengers as well as cargo. On 23 June, for example, she reached Manhattan with 2,987 German prisoners, 313 guards, 920 troops, 678 civilians and 2,654 bags of mail. During the next call, on 17 July, she landed 3,988 prisoners and 468 guards among the 5,060 listed on the manifest. There were also 5,395 bags of mail and 69 boxes of gold on board.

Joseph Fencil was a US Army serviceman in early 1944, when he crossed on the *Queen Mary*:

We had come by train from Camp Shanks, near Orangeburg, New York, to Weehawken, New Jersey, just across from the great passenger ship piers of Manhattan. We had no idea where we were headed, except that it was to England. We were put aboard a New York Central Railroad ferry and, as we began to cross the Hudson at dusk, we saw the big grey ship berthed at Pier 90. She was blacked-out, even in New York. Only then, we knew which ship was to take us across the Atlantic. The ferry docked on the south side of Pier 90 [the *Mary* was in the north berth] and we shuttled across, loading all through the night.

We sailed at nine the next morning and only those who managed to get a porthole could see the Statue [the Statue of Liberty in Lower New York harbour].

I was assigned a bunk, one of those that was eight high. However, some of us took our chances by sleeping on deck, wearing all of our clothes and with blankets. It was a rough trip and the *Mary* took several dives. Her bow would go under and then you could feel the stern section lift out of the sea, the four propellers momentarily churning in mid air. We hit a large piece of ice one night and the thump rattled throughout the ship. Of course, many of the troops were scared throughout the voyage. Myself, I had great confidence in the *Mary*. I knew that her speed was her best defence and that she could outrun almost any attack. We always zigzagged and remained completely blacked-out at night.

We were fed twice a day, breakfast and then dinner. There was no lunch. The food was mostly English — mutton, kidney beans, marmalade and tea. Since there were over 15,000 of us on board, there were not enough showers for our use. I don't recall anyone bathing for the entire five days. We had drills every day. In between, to pass the time, there were some very good card games, played mostly with the English crewmen, who desperately wanted Yankee dollars. Others simply told stories, watched the sea or, for so many, were quite sick most of the time and held fast to the rails.

Our first land sighting was the Irish coast, although this was not officially announced. We had no idea where we were headed. Soon afterward, we reached Gourock. Again, we were loaded into ferries, taken ashore and then put on fast trains to the south of England. I was sent to Lancashire and later went on to France. I returned home finally, in June 1945, aboard the *General Gordon* to Norfolk.

On 5 September 1944, Churchill and his party of 195 were again to use the *Mary* for a special run to Halifax, for another wartime conference at Quebec City. For security reasons, some Dutch-language signs were posted aboard, in rather obvious corridors and passageways, feeding the deliberately planted rumour that exiled Queen Wilhelmina of the Netherlands was travelling, certainly not the Prime Minister. Other rumours were cleverly spread also, under the theory that 'the more stories, the more safety'. Without Churchill on board, attempts by stray U-boats to hit the *Mary* were far less likely. Special quarters were arranged once again and all the main deck was sectioned off. However, on this occasion, the *Mary* would not wait at Halifax. Promptly after landing the 'secret party', she proceeded to New York.

Among the 3,399 other passengers on this sailing were a considerable number of sick and wounded, who were carried on specially fitted medical cots. Many wartime wounded would travel on both Queens in subsequent sailings, all met by squadrons of ambulances and stretcher buses at Pier 90. Although the US Army medical staffs of nearly 100 doctors and nurses were placed aboard each of the Queens in the later years of the war, the Cunard staff often assisted with the feeding and care of the more critically injured, in an outstanding effort of co-operation.

Also on this voyage, for the first time since the war began, the *Mary* went southwards from Gourock through the Irish Sea, then past southern Ireland and finally out into the open Atlantic. In itself, this suggested that the danger from possible enemy attack was diminishing. She sped westward for Halifax at an average speed of 27.86 knots, reaching that port in four days and nineteen hours. Then, after a two-hour call to debark the Churchill party, the liner went to sea again and headed for New York.

Two weeks later, on 20 September, as the *Queen Mary* sailed from Pier 90 carrying 8,888 troops and 196 special passengers, she paused briefly in the Lower Bay, off the Quarantine Station on Staten Island. A Navy tender came alongside to load yet one more passenger, 'the Grand Old Man' himself. Churchill went direct to the bridge to examine the newly installed radar and to discuss the forthcoming homeward voyage to Britain with the liner's master. He later made a loudspeaker speech to the troops. It had been decided that, to save time, the Prime Minister would be landed by tender at Fishguard on the Welsh coast. However, as the *Mary* neared the shore, heavy weather was encountered and Churchill was forced to remain with the ship all the way to Gourock.

At the conclusion of this crossing, a letter was delivered to Commodore Bisset, master of the *Queen Mary*:

My dear Commodore,

Mrs Churchill and I wish to thank you and through you all those who have been concerned in making this voyage so comfortable for ourselves and the members of the Mission.

All the arrangements were quite admirable and the facilities provided enabled the Staffs to continue their duties and get through a great amount of essential work.

We hope that, at some future date, we may again travel in your fine ship.

> Yours sincerely,
> Winston S. Churchill

Beginning in the autumn of 1944, the Queens were outfitted to carry more and more sick and wounded passengers. The alteration work, which normally would have been done in a shipyard, was undertaken while the liners were anchored off Gourock. A steady flow of tenders, work boats and barges relayed shipyard crews, equipment and supplies. It was a cumbersome but unavoidable operation. The Queens still could not be risked in dry dock, even at this late date in the war, and the alternative docks were at heavily bomb-damaged Southampton.

Just before her much needed dry-docking and overhaul at Bayonne, in New York harbour, in November 1944, the *Mary* encountered some of the worst weather of her life. She tossed and rolled, through 23°, and was forced to reduce speed from 28 to 22 knots. Rumour spread that she nearly capsized.

For her first voyages into 1945, the year of 'victory at last', the *Mary* left New York on 18 February with 11,226 troops and then on 17 March with 10,905 more servicemen. Charles F. Trapp of Jersey City, New Jersey was on board that latter crossing:

At sailing, we could sense that the *Queen Mary* was a very crowded ship. There was humanity from end to end.

We had sailed from New York twice on that St Patrick's Day. The first sailing was at 10am, just when a sudden fog came over the River as we reached mid-stream. Bull horns went into action very quickly. A flock of orders came from the bridge to shore. One was for the tugs to get her back into the dock just as the fog grew thicker. While moving her back into Pier 90, the lead fender boom caught fire from the friction applied to it. Then, the *Mary* stopped very short of suddenly colliding with the USS *Illinois*, which was tied up just north of us, at Pier 92. She had being doing duty as a Navy receiving ship. Twelve tugs seemed to come from nowhere and promptly fastened lines to the big Cunarder. I had a grandstand seat throughout the docking procedure.

The second sailing was during that same night and went off very quietly

— absolutely no noise! When I awoke, we were far out to sea. We were quartered in the stern section, well below the waterline, together with some Coast Guard personnel. I felt that if anything ever happened, we would never get out. However, the frequent fire drills left us little time to stay below.

The meals were hardly praiseworthy: mutton, marmalade and tea. We were fed this fare twice per day. The ship was divided into sections for meals: red, white and blue. The 'brass' could buy some extra luxuries that were on board, but not us guys. Piccadilly Square [the officers' canteen] was off limits.

While off Atlantic Canada, we were in a storm for two full days. For a time, she rode quite steady, but at others, she bounced about like a cork. You could hardly believe that the sea was so strong. We were carrying a regiment of black troops and most of them were terribly seasick. What a mess in the companionways, especially near the radiators!

Early on the morning of the 23rd, we anchored in the Firth of Clyde, the only major ship there among twelve 'baby' flat-tops, whose planes were ashore. As we watched the anchors being lowered, we thought that they would never reach bottom. The sounds of the rattling chains seemed endless. This marked the end of our transatlantic crossing. We were shuttled ashore by the side-wheeler *Edward VII*. Once ashore, we were put aboard a 'fast train' with a green light all the way, travelling from Gourock and Glasgow and then arriving the next morning in a rainy Southampton. That night, we were ferried across the Channel aboard the steamer *Altenor* to Le Havre. The journey was complete.

However, despite the near-collapse of the Nazi regime in that late winter and early spring of 1945, crossings in the Queens were still quite tense for many. Dermod J. Kirwan from Limerick was aboard the *Elizabeth* out of New York on 28 February:

We were not escorted until the last day of the six-day voyage. You can understand that I and many others felt rather anxious. With so many soldiers aboard, one's chances of survival would not have been good in the event of an attack. Of course, I said nothing to anyone about this because in wartime it simply wasn't done to express such discouraging thoughts. However, I shared a cabin with a Frenchman named Pierre, who was returning from a lecture tour in Canada. He told me that he had been imprisoned by the Germans early in the war, when they first occupied France. He said that while in prison he was expecting each day to be brought out and shot. Now on board the *Queen Elizabeth*, he was expecting each day to be torpedoed!

Soon after the German surrender on 7 May, the troop figures for the two Queens dropped drastically and suddenly. When the *Mary* sailed from New York on 5 June, bound on her usual course to Gourock, her manifests showed only 1,207 passengers, with no distinguishable troop figures. The black-outs and perpetual zigzagging were eliminated immediately. The tensions, the extra lookouts and the gun patrols of previous crossings were gone. Both the *Mary* and *Elizabeth* were proud, heroic survivors of the great conflict, one in which 4,280 Allied and 490 neutral flagships had been lost. The Queens were now selected, like so many other troopers, to return American and Canadian servicemen. In fact, the *Mary* took the first official American units home, on 15 June, from Gourock. When she reached New York at noon on 20 June, 14,777 GIs took position along every open deck, in every deck locker, in every ventilator and deck passageway — becoming a flood of waving, cheering humanity along those top decks. Flags were waved, sirens and horns blared, whistles thundered and all while harbour boats and overhead aircraft created a grand welcoming escort. Some 130 reporters and photographers were later welcomed aboard the liner at Pier 90. One of them asked Commodore Bisset, 'Is it true that the *Queen Mary* once ran through a pack of twenty-five U-boats?' To this, the smiling commodore replied, 'U-boats are heard, not seen. I didn't want to see them. They wanted to see me!'

The writer Paul Gallico, who had made a wartime crossing on the *Mary*, offered a summing-up of the ship's valiant wartime performance:

I remember her dazzling speed through the submarine zones, and the graceful and easy way she would lean over into the zigzags to frustrate the undersea wolf packs. I remember her for the way she swallowed up 15,000 GIs at a clip, housed and fed and transported them with never a slip . . . and for the wonderful teeming life that filled her during those war crossings, the ceaseless barking of the loudspeakers. Wherever she goes, may fair winds, calm seas and good luck go with her.

4

Post-War and Restoration

When the *Mary* arrived at Gourock on 22 July 1945, disembarking 567 passengers and troops, it was the last time that she would anchor in the Clyde in her wartime role. The hostilities in Europe were over, the threat of air attack or lurking U-boats had passed. At their Liverpool headquarters, Cunard officials were already busy making plans for their peacetime resumption of Atlantic liner service. Among the most important prospects, the *Mary* would finally be joined by the *Elizabeth* on the first-ever two-ship transatlantic express shuttle. Alone, this would lure tens of thousands of passengers, millions in revenue and secure a dominant post-war position for Cunard over the entire trade.

Among the initial decisions was to begin reusing Southampton as the terminal port for the express run. The *Mary* had last been there in August 1939; the *Elizabeth* had never called. The Admiralty assured Cunard that, while relying on strictly prescribed courses, the Channel was sufficiently free of mines in that summer of victory. Almost appropriately, the *Mary* was then first to return to Southampton, when she called on 12 August, landing well over 1,000 passengers. Among them was Crown Princess Juliana of the Netherlands with her daughters, the Princesses Beatrix, Irene and Margriet, who were returning from wartime exile in Canada.

The *Elizabeth* sailed up the Solent and first docked at her new British terminal port one week later, on 20 August. As she was brought into the Ocean Dock the National Anthems of both America and Britain were played and the welcoming crowd fell poignantly silent as she was manoeuvred by the tugs. Later, during an official ceremony held in the main lounge, the Mayor and Mayoress and other local dignitaries offered a toast of thanks to the captain and his crew for bringing 'Southampton's Baby' safely to her home port for the first time. Of course, Liverpool was always listed on her stern as the home port, but to many this was a distinction only for Southampton.

Both Queens were to continue with repatriation work with American and Canadian forces for at least six more months. Now, the westward movement was almost equivalent to the massive flow that had crossed the Atlantic eastbound in the years just passed. However, the sense of urgency, the secrecy, the zigzagging and the black-outs were happily missing. Impressive westbound figures from Southampton throughout the remainder of 1945 were now recorded:

	Sailing	Troops	Total passengers
Queen Mary	6 July*	8,551	
Queen Mary	28 July*	14,790	
Queen Mary	17 August	14,776	
Queen Elizabeth	26 August	14,996	15,850
Queen Mary	5 September	14,803	
Queen Elizabeth	14 September	14,979	15,830
Queen Mary	23 September	14,938	15,933
Queen Elizabeth	4 October	15,077	15,932
Queen Mary	11 October	11,383	12,421
Queen Elizabeth	22 October	12,517	13,381
Queen Mary	4 November	11,483	12,368
Queen Mary	22 November	11,683	12,526
Queen Mary	9 December	11,588	12,434
Queen Elizabeth	22 December	12,404	13,372
Queen Mary	29 December	11,346	12,434

(*These sailings were from Gourock)

When the *Elizabeth* sailed from Southampton for New York on 4 October she carried the greatest number of souls aboard in her career. (The highest figure of all time for any ship still went to the *Mary*, however. She crossed the Atlantic with 16,683 on board in July 1943.)

In stark contrast, were some of the eastbound figures for arrivals at Southampton. The *Mary* arrived on 31 August with 11 troops and 93 passengers, on 18 September with 54 troops and 31 passengers, and on 7 October with 11 troops and 29 passengers.

While she was at New York, in September, the *Elizabeth*'s twin funnels were repainted in Cunard colours: orange-red and black.

This was yet another sign of peace at last. The *Mary*'s three stacks were repainted as well shortly thereafter. However, the hulls and superstructures of both liners remained in drab grey.

On 22 October, the *Elizabeth* left Southampton with 12,517 Canadian troops. The Canadian Government had requested that the liner go to Halifax, thereby delivering the first returning national servicemen on to home soil. Cunard had protested. It was the very strong opinion of several captains of the two Queens that Halifax was quite risky for such large ships. The dock there was not enclosed and therefore open to a swell. In the event of a gale, the liners might range back and forth, breaking their mooring lines and possibly suffering considerable damages. Cunard proposed that Boston be used instead, from where the troops could then be trained to Canada. At least for the first homebound run, the Canadian Government wouldn't hear of it. The *Elizabeth* went to Halifax, arriving there on 26 October to a great, cheering welcome. Commander Anthony Keasbey recalled seeing her at the time: 'I could peer down one street and see one funnel, then walk to the next street and look down at the second stack.' She returned to Southampton with 1,820 passengers, including the Canadian Prime Minister, Vincent Massey. But, thereafter, she (and the *Mary* as well) would go only to the Nova Scotia port in extreme emergency. Subsequent Canadian forces would be landed at New York.

Once back at Southampton, the *Elizabeth* took her first turn in the giant King George V Graving Dock, a stay that lasted from 6 November until 20 December, and that would become her wintertime custom. She was at sea over Christmas 1945, bound for New York in a vicious Atlantic storm as her catering department served 13,272 holiday dinners. Eastbound, she spent New Year's Eve at sea, with 1,091 passengers, including Mrs Eleanor Roosevelt, wife of the late President, who was with a special delegation headed for a United Nations Organization Conference in London.

Although the Queens were very much still troopships, some VIP civilian passengers could be accommodated in a reserved part of first class, occupying some of the original suites and larger staterooms. On 9 January 1946, along with 12,314 homebound Canadian troops, such special passengers boarded at Southampton. Winston Churchill and Mrs Churchill were to cross on the *Elizabeth* for the first time, destined for New York en route to a winter holiday in Florida. Churchill, wearing a yachting outfit and cap, went on board just one hour before sailing and immediately up to the bridge. On the last day at sea, he made a stirring speech over the liner's loudspeaker system:

My friends and shipmates in the *Queen Elizabeth*!

For most of you, it is homeward-bound. It has been a good voyage in a great ship, with a fine Captain — or indeed Commodore [Commodore James Bisset]. We have not got there yet, but I am quite sure he will find the way all right. At any rate, he has been over the track before, and, as I can testify myself, having been several times with him, in those days there used to be U-boats and things like that. They all seem to have dropped off now and we don't have to worry about them at all. Something has happened. The seas are clear, the old flag flies, and those who have done the work, or some of it — because the British did some — turn home again, their task accomplished and their duty done.

What a strange, fearful, yet glittering chapter this war has been! What changes it has wrought throughout the world and in the fortunes of so many families! What an interruption in all the plans each of us had made! What a surrender of the liberties we prized! What a casting away of comfort and safety! What a pride in peril! What a glory shines on the brave and true! The good cause has not been overthrown. Tyrants have been hurled from their place of power, and those who sought to enslave the future of mankind have paid, or will pay, the final penalty.

You Canadians, many of whom served in the Canadian 5th Division, no doubt have your minds filled with the victorious war scenes of Italy and the Rhine. But we Englishmen always think of the days of 1940, when the Canadian Army Corps stood almost alone in Kent and Sussex, and the Germans had twenty-five divisions ready to leap across the Channel and wipe Great Britain out of life and history. I think about those days, too, sometimes, and how fine it was to see everyone, at home and throughout the

A small army of 'Mrs Mops' invaded the Queens at Gourock after each troop crossing. In this view they are seen scrubbing the C Deck Square on the *Mary* in 1944 (*Frank O. Braynard Collection*)

A wartime view from the *Queen Mary*'s port bridge wing. Note the guns placed atop the ventilators (*Imperial War Museum*)

Empire, moved by the same impulse, so simple, so sublime — 'Conquer or die!'

Victory in arms, or in any walk of life, is only the opportunity of doing better on a larger scale and a higher level. Do not be anxious about the future! Be vigilant, be strong, be clear-sighted, but do not be worried. Our future is in our hands. Our lives are what we choose to make them. The great British Commonwealth and Empire, emerging from the fire once again, glorious and free, will form a structure and an organisation within which there will be room for all, and a fair chance for all.

Yesterday I was on the bridge, watching the mountainous waves, and this ship — which is no pup — cutting through them and mocking their anger. I asked myself, why is it the ship beats the waves, when they are so many and the ship one? The reason is that the ship has a purpose, and the waves have none. They just flop around, innumerable, tireless, but ineffective. The ship with the purpose takes us where we want to go.

Let us therefore have purpose, both in our national and imperial policy, and in our private lives. Thus the future will be fruitful for each and for all, and the reward of the warriors will not be unworthy of the deeds they have done.

The *Elizabeth*'s subsequent eastbound run had another valuable passenger: the Magna Carta in a tin box. It was the Lincoln Copy, one of four, that had been sent across in the *Queen Mary* in August 1939 for the New York World's Fair. During the war, it had been kept in a vault at Fort Knox in Kentucky for safety. The *Elizabeth*'s master decided to keep the prized historic item in his own cabin, under his bed. He was to pronounce later: 'It's the most precious cargo ever carried in the *Queen Elizabeth*, except the 750,000 troops that have voyaged to and fro in her!'

It was decided that the *Elizabeth* and the old *Aquitania*, persistently sailing since 1914, would finish Atlantic trooping for the British while the *Mary* would remain somewhat longer for the Americans. In fact, in view of her great age, the *Aquitania* was never again fully restored. She finished her sailing days at the end of 1949

The *Mary* with returning servicemen onboard, at Pier 90, New York *(Frank O. Braynard Collection)*

Returning the forces: the *Queen Elizabeth* steams for New York with over 15,000 troops onboard in September 1945 *(Frank O. Braynard Collection)* and then went to Scotland to be scrapped, concluding a thirty-five-year career. It was also decided that the *Queen Elizabeth* would be the first of the two Queens to be restored for peacetime passenger operations.

When the *Elizabeth* reached Southampton on 6 March, she disembarked her last 'wartime service' passengers, 1,709 in all. At berth 101, which had been specially dredged for her, the crew was paid off, and sent on a well-deserved holiday. Only a maintenance staff of about 300 remained. One of the biggest shipboard transformations was about to begin. It was decided that the liner would be converted in familiar wartime waters, at the Tail of the Bank, near the mouth of the Clyde. She was, of course, far too big to navigate the narrow and shallow waters of the upper Clyde to reach her original birthplace, the John Brown yards. For the final phase of this refit, she would return to Southampton for extensive dry-docking before making her first commercial sailing in early October, her maiden voyage of sorts, over six years after that secret crossing in the winter of 1940.

Two days later, on 8 March, in the early hours of daylight, a fire erupted that nearly destroyed the *Elizabeth*. It broke out in a small compartment on the promenade deck. It had been a storage room for drugs, bandages, medical equipment and other highly flammable materials. A bottle of medical alcohol had broken and filled the space with fumes. A workman, breaking rules at the time, sought the area for a quiet cigarette. The fire quickly spread. Complicating matters, the storage area was one of the very few spaces on board that was not fitted with an automatic sprinkler system. Furthermore, the ship's entire fire brigade was ashore. Smoke poured out from the promenade deck area. After so many daring wartime exploits, could the *Queen Elizabeth* be destroyed by fire in peaceful home waters?

The Southampton Fire Brigade was summoned and arrived within minutes. Unfortunately, their ladders were too short to reach the liner's smoky decks. In response, several of the Queen's lifeboats were lowered to the pierside and then rehoisted, carrying firemen and their hoses. Direct jets of water were then aimed into the opened portholes. This persistent blaze lasted for three hours, the closest occasion in her Cunard history that the liner ever came to being completely destroyed.

The fire caused considerable damage, including some flooding, and warped several large steel beams that supported the boat deck. Part of the deck above became a huge blister. Sabotage was never completely ruled out, at least in the minds of many. Thereafter, fire security brigades were increased and the director of the Southampton Docks considered having troops to guard the terminals. After all, the *Queen Mary* was due the next day, the *Aquitania* in the following week, and docked quite close to the *Elizabeth* at the time of the fire were the *Île de France, Pasteur, Andes, Alcantara* and *Athlone Castle*.

The *Elizabeth* eventually left Southampton and anchored off the Clyde on 31 March. At the time, her reconversion was the greatest yet undertaken and assuredly the largest ever for such a vessel at anchor rather than at dock. To many, particularly some of the foremen at the John Brown yards, this was a more complex task than the original construction. So much had to be sorted and then deciphered, so much had been installed at various times and odd places during the war and so much was still in storage. Complicating matters was the steady but cumbersome relay of materials and workers by train and lorry from Clydebank to Gourock and then by barge and tender out to the anchored liner. Some 2,000 workers were involved directly in the project.

The *Elizabeth* maintained steam at all times, should an emergency arise. Much of the heavy wartime equipment was removed and lowered into barges alongside. Over 200 painters and scrapers, dangling in small bosuns' chairs, chipped off the wartime grey, applied a fresh anti-corrosive and then 30 tons of commercial paint for the peacetime colouring. The twenty-six lifeboats were removed and taken, in groups resembling trains, to Gourock for complete restoration. They returned fresh and white.

The innards became a mass of ladders, scaffolding and work tables. All of the linoleum had to be relaid in both the passenger and crew spaces. The 2,000 portholes and windows were scraped clean of black-out paint. Over 4,000 miles of electrical wiring had to be

93

surveyed, sometimes replaced and then carefully tested. The galleys had to be largely rebuilt. The boilers, refrigerators, pantries, storerooms, winches, lifts, cargo equipment and even the clocks had to be renewed.

A special fire security brigade of over 200 kept rigid watch over the ship, especially after the Southampton incident. Furthermore, there was widespread use of acetylene torches and electrical welding, and it had been sparks from an acetylene torch that started the fatal fire aboard the *Normandie* at New York four years before.

Some of the *Elizabeth*'s original furnishings, which had been fitted in 1939, were simultaneously brought home to Britain. The materials that had been stored in America arrived at Southampton on the *Aquitania*; that from Australia came by freighter to Liverpool and was temporarily stored at Pilsworth in Lancashire. Other items — such as chairs, tables and carpets, which had never even been put aboard the ship — were already in handy storages at Southampton, Woolston and at Brockenhurst and Lymington in the New Forest. All of this was later taken to rented hangars (totalling some 90,000sq ft) at Southampton Airport at Eastleigh for systematic sorting, refurbishing and grouping. The largest hangar space was used for sorting and identification, the smallest hangar for workers and restorers from John Brown's, and the remainder of the space as both a workshop and accommodation centre. This massive project involved over 21,000 pieces of furniture and equipment — more specifically, over 4,500 settees, chairs and tables, 4,000 mattresses, 6,000 curtains and bedspreads, 2,000 carpets and 1,500 wardrobes and dressing tables.

The *Elizabeth* returned to Southampton on 16 June, for the second and final phase of her conversion. On 6 August, she entered the King George V Graving Dock for her underwater refit. Over 1,000 workers from John Brown's — carpenters, plumbers, joiners, electricians, painters, fitters, designers and other artisans — went to Southampton to complete the task of restoring the *Elizabeth*. Many were housed in a Nissen hut camp site at Chandler's Ford, quite near to the Southampton Docks, and then bussed to the ship itself. Along the pier, a mammoth dockside canteen was created, serving over 2,000 meals each day.

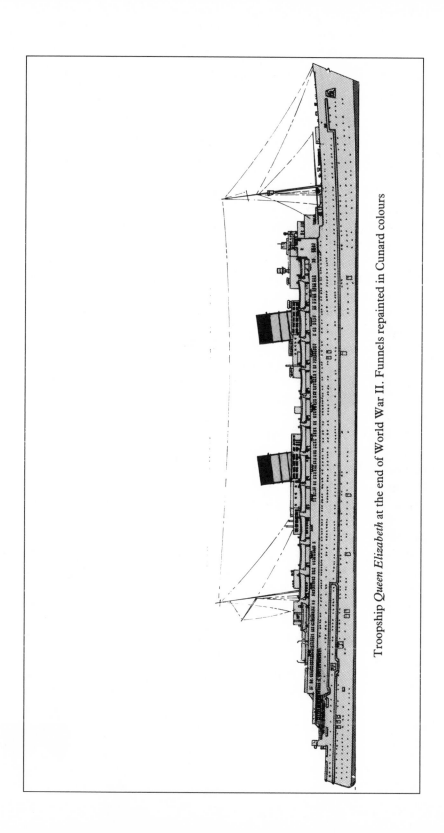

Troopship *Queen Elizabeth* at the end of World War II. Funnels repainted in Cunard colours

The restoration of the *Elizabeth* became very symbolic, much like the completion of the *Mary* had been in the bleak years of the Depression. To Cunard, the new Queen was 'the wonder ship', the finest ocean liner in the world, certainly the most luxurious.

The British Government was even more enthusiastic about the *Elizabeth*'s completion. To them, she would demonstrate to the world Britain's determination to 'win the peace'. She was the grand floating symbol of the 'new British age', reminding Americans, Europeans and the rest of the Empire of 'peace at last'. In reality, of course, while the two Queens were being beautifully reappointed with glistening veneers, large soft chairs and well-provisioned restaurants (supplied, in fact, mostly from the American side), Britain had slipped into an austerity, and end-of-war gloom that was worse even than that during the conflict itself. Rationing, queues and shortages were more common than ever. Politically, the Empire itself was about to begin its sad decline, which would be sparked by the loss of India. The Queens were merely tonics, dispensed mostly in press reports, to a weary Britain. At best, they would provide comfortable transport for visitors from across the Atlantic — either to England, where cities in the late forties still had much and very noticeable bomb and fire ruin, or to the Continent, through Cherbourg, where a ravaged Europe was slowly reawakening.

During August and September of 1946, the press were invited to tour the *Elizabeth* as she completed her refit at Southampton. Newspapers carried enthusiastic and detailed stories of her magnificence and wonder. Through the use of lighter woods the *Elizabeth* appeared more modern than the original *Mary*. Overall, there seemed a finer sense of spaciousness. The *Mary* always appeared the older ship that she was. However, exactly what was original for the *Elizabeth* (from 1939–40) and what was changed (in 1946) has never been clearly determined. Cunard never revealed the changes, if any, that might have occurred between those seven or so years. Certainly, post-war tastes were different. To many, the *Elizabeth* — while always a delightful ship — was not quite as grand as the *Mary*. Many felt that the former ship's décor reflected, in fact, the post-war austerity of Britain, no matter how subtly.

96

Descriptions of the decoration on the *Elizabeth* could fill pages and, indeed, did. The walls in the first-class salon were covered in quilted satin while the secluded verandah grill featured ivory-coloured veneers. The first-class main lounge had a magnificent marquetry panel of coloured woods entitled 'The Canterbury Pilgrims'. The cabin-class indoor pool was lined in mosaic tile while the walls included medallions of sea creatures. There was a squash court on the sports deck and a fully-equipped gymnasium. Thirty-five elevators linked the ship's thirteen passenger decks. All of the first-class suites and staterooms were fitted with telephones that could be linked to most of the world's major cities. Thirty-six different design themes were used in the creation of these rooms. On the rear wall of the first-class restaurant was a clock surrounded by lime-wood carvings of the signs of the Zodiac. Overall, the room could comfortably seat 850, all of the first-class passengers at one time.

Press releases, booklets and brochures revealed seemingly endless facts and statistics about the liner. For example, there were 680 telephones on board, 30,000 lamps, 700 clocks, 37 public rooms and 257,000 turbine blades. There were 4 propellers, each weighing 32 tons and measuring 18ft in diameter. Each of the 3 steam whistles, weighing 1 ton, could be heard for 10 miles. The two power stations could light an equivalent city of 30,000 residents. Even the name letters on the bow were subject to enumeration: the fourteen letters were each 2½ft high and covered a distance of 68ft.

Proportionally, the *Elizabeth* was five times the length of the first Cunarder, the 207-ft long *Britannia* of 1840. She was 50ft taller, if placed on end, than the Eiffel Tower and just shorter than the world's second tallest skyscraper, New York's 1,046-ft Chrysler Building. She was three times the height of St Paul's in London.

On 6 October, the *Elizabeth* was ready for her trials, those tests which never quite happened in February 1940, just before she secretly crossed to New York. She went from Southampton to the Firth of Clyde for these special runs. On 7 October — with the chairmen of both Cunard and John Brown's, and the Minister of Transport on board — she made two unofficial sprints at over 30 knots without great strain; official trials would come on the next day.

Sir Percy Bates, the Cunard chairman, went ashore that morning of 8 October to personally greet three distinguished guests: Her Majesty Queen Elizabeth and Their Royal Highnesses the Princesses Elizabeth and Margaret, who had enthusiastically accepted the invitation to join the liner for the sea trials. The Royal party was ceremoniously greeted at the Gourock Pier and then travelled in the Clyde steamer *Queen Mary II* (renamed from simply *Queen Mary* in the mid-thirties in deference to the Cunarder) to board the *Elizabeth* at anchor. The Queen's standard was broken at the mainmast head.

At first, the Royals — accompanied by other officials, guests, and a small army from the press — toured the liner's recently completed passenger interiors. Then they went to the bridge to witness the 'measured mile' runs. Each of the Princesses was given a stop watch. The liner covered the first measured mile in 2 minutes, 1.3 seconds, at a speed of 29.71 knots, and then the second mile in 2 minutes, 1 second, at 29.75 knots. The liner was then swung round in a full circle and headed south for two more measured mile runs. This time, Queen Elizabeth herself took the wheel, carefully advised by the Cunard commodore. The ship made each of the miles in exactly 2 minutes, precisely at 30 knots. Everyone was absolutely thrilled and delighted. By the late afternoon, the Royals returned to Gourock by tender.

On 9 October, the *Elizabeth* took on 400 VIP guests for the short passage back to Southampton, where she was finally to begin her commercial service to New York. Steaming southward in the Irish Sea, a British submarine surfaced and flashed, 'What a beautiful target!' To which Commodore Bisset responded, 'I've been thinking that too, ever since I sighted you.' Later, an aged and well-loaded collier, creeping along at a scant 6 knots, signalled to the liner: 'What ship are you?'

The maiden voyage began on 16 October, from Southampton to New York via Cherbourg. Over 7,000 had requested space for the crossing, but only an absolute maximum of 2,288 were accepted in the end. This was fifty-five above her listed cabin capacity, but the additional spaces were created by using cots and some beds in the hospital. There were four boat trains down from London. Some of her passengers had been waiting from as early as 1938, when they had booked for the proposed April 1940 maiden crossing. Several others had sailed in her during the war and now wanted the opportunity to make her first luxury passage. Cunard claimed that its first post-war fare-paying passenger had, in fact, sailed on the *Elizabeth* in August 1945, from Gourock to New York. He had paid $200 for the voyage and was alone in the tender that delivered him to the otherwise troop-filled liner. A Long Island, New York businessman, he later recalled, 'What a pleasant trip. We passed some German U-boats waiting to surrender.'

Among the passengers on the 1946 maiden run, which was to hint at so many first-class rosters in the years ahead, were three ambassadors, three newspaper tycoons, two Members of Parliament, four dance band leaders and assorted industrialists. Also along was the Foreign Minister of Czechoslovakia, US Senator Tom Connally, writer Ludwig Bemelmans, cosmetic queen Helena Rubinstein and two quite secretive government ministers from Soviet Russia — Messrs M. Molotov and M. Vyshinsky. Remaining mostly in their B deck suite, the two Russians were surrounded by guards and a special shipboard security patrol. At one point, Mr Molotov was invited to the bridge and, as a courtesy gesture, took the wheel of the liner for a short time. As the *Elizabeth* sped from New York, her owners and staff could enjoy the fact that she was almost fully booked for the next twelve months and that her running-mate, the *Queen Mary*, would join her on the Atlantic shuttle by the mid-summer of 1947.

The *Queen Mary* had been running something of a post-war austerity service to New York throughout 1946, in company with the aged *Aquitania* and the second *Mauretania*. Of course, this was only temporary, until she could eventually work in tandem with the *Elizabeth*. Throughout most of 1946, the *Mary* continued to repatriate American servicemen and she carried some civilian passengers as well. Often, she arrived at New York with the same high numbers on board that she had sailed eastbound with during the war. Somewhere, it was calculated that the post-war cost was $80.70 per serviceman for passage in the ship. However, this was determined simply for accounting purposes.

The American War Department issued some figures on 15 March 1946, covering a period between March 1940 and September 1945 for both Queens. During that time, some 902,611 Americans were carried aboard the liners, both on the North Atlantic and even out to Australia, at a total cost of $90,877,750. This figure, it can be assumed, was for the provisioning, refuelling and repairing of the liners as well as a determined minimum fare per serviceman that was a cost to the US Government.

In an article in the *New York Herald Tribune*, dated 18 October 1946, Vice Admiral William W. Smith, then chairman of the American Maritime Commission, was quoted as saying that the US Government paid 'more than $1 million a trip' for the wartime voyages on which the *Queen Mary* and *Queen Elizabeth* carried American troops. Combined, the two liners made over fifty wartime voyages, which, at over $1 million per trip, could easily have reached the $90.8 million announced by the War Department. Cunard claimed not to have made any great profit on either of the Queens during the war and that the whole cost of operating the ships was born by the British Government.

The *Queen Mary* saw particularly strenuous service as a 'war bride ship' in those early months of 1946. She is reputed to have carried 30 per cent of all British girls who had married American soldiers and who were now permitted to go to the States under a special government scheme. In all, she carried 12,886 brides plus 1,683 children and 2,085 infants.

Special cots, and washing and ironing rooms were set up. American Red Cross nurses arranged special stations in the lounges. Appropriate lifebelts were made for the youngsters and even a collapsible chair was created to fit into the adult-sized dining room chairs. Lectures and socials were held to acquaint English women with the American way of life. It was something of a reverse of the instructions given to the GIs going to Britain for the first time during the war. There was even a very noticeable offering of coffee rather than tea. It was, of course, quite deliberate, another attempt to familiarise British women with American habits. President Truman was so moved by this special duty of the *Queen Mary* and her unique passengers that, during a tugboat strike at New York, he personally ordered eight Army tugs to dock the liner at Pier 90.

During the summer of 1946, the *Mary* also began to carry Canadian brides and children. Then, finally, on 29 September 1946, arriving at Southampton from Halifax, her war work was officially over. She was demobilised. With her three funnels in Cunard colours but her superstructure and hull still in drab grey, she passed the nearly complete *Elizabeth*, resting regally at the New Docks and only three weeks away from her post-war maiden voyage.

The *Mary*'s record was very impressive: a total of 810,730 wartime passengers (mostly service personnel) in over 500,000 miles. For the *Elizabeth*, the statistics stood at 811,324 personnel and over 492,000 miles. In all, Cunard ships had carried 2.4 million wartime passengers, of which 1.2 million went aboard the Queens. The company had entered the war with eighteen passenger ships. By 1945, there were only nine, excluding the *Georgic*, which by then was only managed by the company for the Ministry of Transport.

In a change of plans, it was decided that the *Mary* would be restored at Southampton rather than at the anchorage off Gourock used by the *Elizabeth*. Again, the sorting, identification and final installation of over 20,000 items was a massive, often nerve-twisting operation. Some 10,000 pieces of furniture had to be brought to the rented hangars at Southampton Airport from New York, Australia and from the nearby New Forest. Two hundred cases of furniture came home aboard the *Mary* herself from New York. Even a new bow section, that had been built as a spare at Boston after the *Curacoa* collision, was delivered to Southampton in the liner. It was later fitted in the King George V Graving Dock.

For a time, the interiors of the *Mary* were bare, steel shells as workers carried out restorations, repairs and surveys, checked wiring and plumbing, and even made some improvements. Several aspects of the accommodation on the *Elizabeth* were considered far superior to those on the *Mary* and therefore Cunard chose this time to make the latter ship more compatible and more modern. A separate cinema was created as well as several new lounges and a cocktail bar. Even the shopping centre was improved, with new fluorescent lighting. At times, there were over 3,000 workers (including 120 French polishers) on board. A special fire security staff was again on constant patrol, and a special ship's police force was arranged to discourage pilferage.

Sparkling with fresh paint, the *Mary* left from Southampton on 24 July 1947, for a mini-cruise of tests and trials. She returned to a specially arranged meeting off Cowes with the *Elizabeth*. For the first time, the two Queens were in sight of each other dressed in their commercial colours. Their throaty whistles, bellowing in salute and acknowledgement, were heard for miles.

On 31 July, the *Mary* sailed from Southampton and Cherbourg on her first post-war commercial voyage to New York. This sailing, like so many ahead, was fully booked — 1,957 passengers in all — and included some who had been on her maiden run eleven years before, in May 1936.

The post-war Cunard liner fleet was the biggest on the Atlantic. No company could offer more sailings, more berths or ships of better repute. In those years, Cunard was a legend, its ships superb. Indeed, as the company slogan enthusiastically pronounced, 'getting there was half the fun!'

The Queens, as intended, maintained the express run between Southampton and New York with a stop at Cherbourg in each direction. The formula worked for two full decades. Generally, they sailed from Southampton on Thursdays, crossed the Channel and then made their brief call at the French port (it was tender service only until 1952). Then, they headed for the open Atlantic and raced across to New York, reaching that end customarily on Tuesdays. At Manhattan's Pier 90, they had a basic, but very busy twenty-four-hour turnaround. On Wednesdays, they would sail again, with a new load of passengers and a full supply of provisions and fuel, for the eastward leg of their transoceanic circuit.

The Queens worked to a precision timetable, with very few deviations especially in those early years. It was useful to tens of thousands of sea travellers — the diplomats and film stars, the industrialists and especially the more simple tourists — to know that there was a weekly departure for most of the year on two large, world-famed, very fast, safe, and comfortable 'floating cities'.

The passengers accommodation on the Queens was balanced in three classes, the normal arrangement for most major liners after the war. Berthing on the *Elizabeth* was organised between 823 in first class; 662 in cabin class, which Cunard spiritedly advertised as 'the happy medium'; and 798 in tourist class — for a total of 2,283. The *Mary*'s accommodation was put at 711 in first, 707 in cabin and 577 in tourist — a total of 1,995. Minimum one-way fares for the 1949 season were listed as £130 in first class, £80 in cabin and £59 for tourist.

At its peak, in the mid-fifties, Cunard was said to be carrying a third of all passengers that crossed the North Atlantic. Their prime year was 1957, when there were twelve Cunard liners in service: the *Queen Elizabeth, Queen Mary, Mauretania, Caronia, Britannic, Media, Parthia, Scythia, Saxonia, Ivernia, Carinthia* and *Sylvania*.

However, soon after, life slowly began to change for both the Queens and Cunard itself. A new, quite different competitor had arrived: the jet. Travel time across the Atlantic suddenly changed from six days to six hours. Cunard managers were initially hostile, thinking that travel in such new, comparatively uncomfortable craft was just a fad. After all, so they thought, 'real travellers' would still prefer the Queens. Within a year after the first commercial jet flight to London in October 1958, the airline industry had secured 63 per cent of all European passenger traffic — 1,539,934 by air against 881,894 by sea. This trend intensified steadily.

5

Epilogue for the
Mary and *Elizabeth*

In the spring of 1966, the British Merchant Marine came to a halt for seven weeks. It was one of the worst and most damaging strikes ever, one that would have many far-reaching effects. Alone, it would help to cast a deciding blow to the future of the Queens. At Southampton, a large, idle fleet — one that would never be seen again in such numbers — waited at various docks and moorings. Among the passenger ships were the *Mary* and *Elizabeth*, the *Carmania, Franconia, Caronia, Southern Cross, Capetown Castle, Pendennis Castle, Edinburgh Castle, Reina del Mar, Windsor Castle, SA Vaal, SA Oranje, Andes, Canberra, Arcadia, Camito* and *Golfito*. The strike cost some £330,000 per week with an overall final estimate put at £4 million. Even when the situation was finally settled in June, earnings for all passenger lines were severely limited. Cunard had already lost £14.1 million between 1961 and 1965 on its passenger division. What could the future hold?

The Queens had first begun to fall in the 'red' in 1961, less than three years after the first commercial jet crossing. However, the problem primarily lay with the ships themselves. The old, impeccable image was hard hit by some new, far flashier Atlantic competition — namely the likes of the *France, Rotterdam* and *Leonardo da Vinci*. It was a repeat of the situation that had finished off the old *Mauretania* and *Berengaria* in the Thirties as the trendy *Bremen* and *Normandie* sailed into service. Furthermore, the two Cunarders were hardly suited for anything but the North Atlantic. For most other Atlantic ships, winter cruising had become a very important, profit-making alternative.

By February 1963, however, the company finally glanced at sunshine cruising for the rather desperate Queens. The *Elizabeth* was sent on a five-day junket from New York to Nassau (where she could only anchor offshore because of her great size), with fares beginning at $125. The mood on board had changed — from those earlier days of dukes and duchesses in the main lounge to parties of retired shoe salesmen from Rochester and garden club groups from Cincinnati. In December of that same year, the *Mary* went on her first cruise (and the first for Cunard from Britain since 1939), from Southampton to Las Palmas and back. For many, these short runs, competitively priced, were a last chance to sail aboard the famous Queens.

More one-class voyages followed, both to Nassau and Las Palmas, and then one large-scale romp for the *Mary* from New York to Las Palmas, Tangier, Piraeus, Naples, Cannes, Gibraltar and Lisbon. But, of course, the aged Queens were quite out of step with the cruise trade, 'limping leviathans', as *The Times* called them. They lacked full air-conditioning and outdoor pools (so essential in the tropics) and, for the Americans, there were too many cabins without private facilities. Newer, sleek white-hulled cruise ships lured the better part of this holiday business. On the Atlantic, while the summer voyages grew less and less plentiful (and profitable), the winters became a hideous nightmare. Cunard persisted in maintaining something of a regular service, even in the middle of frigid January and February. The old liners rattled and moaned across their familiar route, but mostly with silent lounges and long, empty corridors. On at least one occasion, the *Elizabeth* steamed into New York harbour in mid-winter with less than 200 passengers on board, disproportionately serviced by over 1,100 crewmembers! In the mid-fifties, when Cunard earned as much as £7 million per year in profits, such 'traditionalist' sailings were possible; but in the middle sixties, such trips were pure lunacy. By the end of 1966, the Queens were each losing as much as £750,000 annually.

One effort to reprieve at least one of the pair, the *Elizabeth*, had been attempted during an extended £1 million winter refit in 1965–66. A full lido deck and pool were built in the stern section, air-conditioning and private toilets and showers extended to most of the liner, and all with the result that the twenty-five-year-old ship would last another ten years, until 1975, as an early partner to the new Queen, that had just been ordered from John Brown's to replace the *Mary*. But this scheme foundered as well. The *Elizabeth* — her regal, class-divided image still intact — could not quite make the successful transition to tropic fun ship. And again, further cruise ships, especially in the more competitive American lines, were securing the bulk of the trade. Then also, the Queens suffered from increasing operational costs — expensive labour, rising fuel costs and more frequent maintenance in their old ages. The royal pair were often scarred with rust, the service wasn't as prompt and those grand menus weren't quite as grand. Cunard had reached financially fragile times, and it showed.

On 9 May 1967, the bitter news was flashed around the world: 'The Chairman of Cunard yesterday pronounced the death sentence on the two most famous ships the world has known.' The demise of the thirty-one-year-old *Mary* was somehow expected, but that the *Elizabeth* would go as well seemed devastating. The *Mary* would make her exit almost immediately, in September, while the *Elizabeth* would go in October of the following year.

The immediate fate of the *Queen Mary* caused endless speculation and rumour. An Australian syndicate was said to want her for the Southampton-to-Sydney immigrant run. The City of New York wanted her for use as a tourist attraction and then as a public high school, in Brooklyn no less. Another scheme was to make her into a floating hotel at Gibraltar. Even the scrappers bid for her. Sentimentalists proposed that she should stay at home in British waters, at best at the Southampton Ocean Terminal, as a museum of the great era of

The *Queen Elizabeth* at anchor off the Tail of the Bank, Scotland, in the early summer of 1946. Work boats and tugs are huddled alongside the liner's side while painters dangle from bosun's chairs to perform the paint chipping and then repainting. Notice that all of the ship's lifeboats are temporarily missing, having gone to Greenock for full restoration (*Frank O. Braynard Collection*)

Vertical girders and cross-bracing for the after heli-pad fill a swimming pool on the *QE2* with a forest of steel; a section of pad has already been laid. A naval constructor had gone round the ship after requisitioning, followed by a workman with a cutting torch, deciding where the ship was to be mutilated to facilitate the fitting of the pads (*Southern Newspapers plc, Southampton*)

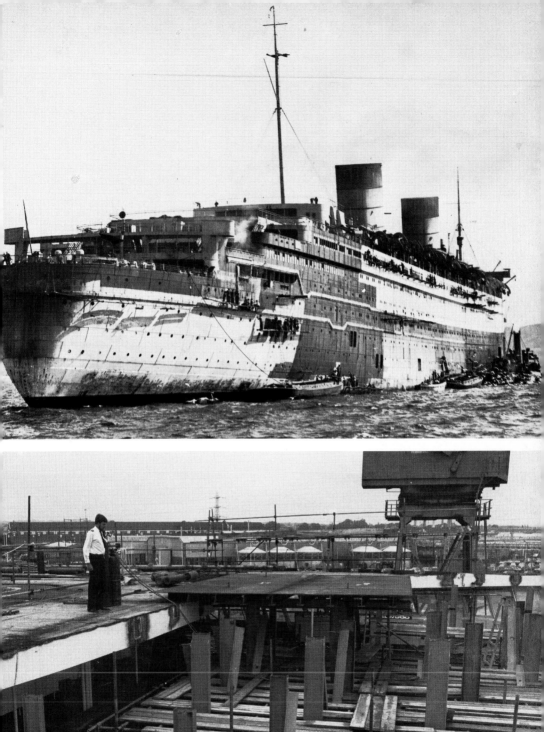

the transatlantic liner. In the end, the City of Long Beach, California — very rich in harbour oil revenues — got her for $3.45 million for use as a tourist gimmick: a combination museum, hotel, convention centre and carnival of shops.

The beloved old *Mary* began her 1,001st Atlantic crossing, from New York, on 22 September 1967 at noon. At an average speed of 27.86 knots she made Southampton on 27 September and landed her last Cunard passengers. Thirty-one years had passed since that maiden voyage, during which she carried over 2 million fare-paying passengers and steamed more than 3 million miles. It was now nearly all over.

Fugazy Travel of New York had chartered the ship for one last sentimental run — a thirty-nine-day trip to Lisbon, Las Palmas, Rio de Janeiro, Valparaiso, Callao, Balboa, Acapulco and then Long Beach. Cunard, while still the official owners, sensibly withdrew to the background. It was an uncomfortable voyage caused mostly by the lack of air-conditioning and the depressed mood among the reduced staff. One couple baled out at Rio and then indiscreetly told the press that the *Mary* was 'a nightmare of rats and roaches'.

The *Mary* reached her new California home on 9 December, forty days and some 14,500 miles out of Southampton. A great flotilla of serenading craft — so similar to the spectacles of 1936 — had welcomed the liner. Two days later, she was officially transferred to City ownership and struck from the British Register of Ships. She underwent a long and very thorough facelift, costing upwards of $72 million, that would suit both her new purpose and the strict American Coast Guard standards. With her propellers and engines no longer operative, she even lost her status as a ship. Technically, she is now classed as a 'building'.

1st Battalion, the 7th Duke of Edinburgh's Own Gurkha Rifles embarking on the *QE2* on the morning of 12 May, 1982. The Gurkhas' own priest chanted prayers as they boarded *(Southern Newspapers plc, Southampton)*

Photographed from one of her helicopters, the *QE2* steams south. Flying operations occurred daily, giving the troops practice in disembarking by helicopter should sea conditions prohibit landing by boat *(Imperial War Museum)*

The Hotel *Queen Mary* opened in May 1971, to mixed reviews. Some were delighted that she had been saved and could still be seen, even if in a less splendid state; others were less enthusiastic, thinking only of the souvenir stands and hamburger vendors that now lined her upper decks. In her first year, the *Mary* welcomed a very encouraging 1.4 million visitors. However, by the end of 1976, this figure had slumped to a mere 450,000. One magazine sarcastically reported 'that every California school child had seen the *Queen Mary* at least twice'. The City of Long Beach was not impressed. By the end of 1978, there were some frightening rumours that she was for sale, possibly for scrapping. Newspaper reports continued to emphasise the *Mary*'s problems. She was simply not a profit-making project. Most often, she lost potential visitors and hotel guests to the many other attractions in southern California.

By the end of 1980, the City fathers at Long Beach found the *Mary*'s future difficult to justify. First, it was arranged for the Wrather Corporation to take over the management and then later to buy the ship outright. By the summer of 1982, Wrather officials were spending some $10 million to rejuvenate the liner, which included her first overall coat of paint in a decade. A new surrounding complex was developed, which included the acquisition of the 'Spruce Goose', the famed flying boat designed by the late Howard Hughes. The *Mary* was given renewed life, a better opportunity to continue in her role as the greatest museum of the age of the ocean liner. Hopefully, she will continue for many years to come.

The *Elizabeth* saw one last season on the Atlantic and then sailed away from New York forever in October 1968. She too was given a gala send-off of surrounding craft, but greater numbers had, in fact, come out for the *Mary* thirteen months before. The *Queen Mary* was always the more beloved of the two liners. She had the more successful life: a pre-war career, the Blue Riband, an illustrious war record and then generally profitable service thereafter. She was also, at least according to many opinions at Cunard, the better ship to run. The *Elizabeth* never had the same fine rapport with her staff that the *Mary* had enjoyed for all of her life.

The Queen Mother had asked to see the *Queen Elizabeth* once more, before the ship sailed for a new career. As graciously as ever, she inspected the liner that she had named thirty years before. However, it was reported that only one side of the *Elizabeth* was freshly painted for the occasion, the side that Her Majesty would see.

The *Elizabeth* did not have the benefit or glory of a dignified retirement. After her final Cunard voyage in November 1968, she sailed to Port Everglades, Florida (Philadelphia had first been proposed), supposedly to become the East Coast version of what the *Mary* was to be in southern California, living out her remaining days as a hotel, convention centre, museum and shopping mall.

Although there was never an official relationship between the two ventures and while Cunard retained an 85 per cent share in the *Elizabeth*, the project was clouded from the start by all sorts of difficulties, not the least of which were financial woes and mismanagement. Amidst palm trees and under a scorching sun, the *Elizabeth* seemed unwanted (and mostly unattended) for nearly two years. Her hull was streaked in even more rust, her funnels faded and her vast open decks weathered badly. Her long corridors and empty lounges grew musty and tomb-like. The project would never come to be.

During the summer of 1970, the *Elizabeth* was put on the auction block. C. Y. Tung of Taiwan, then a member of the world's new generation of shipping tycoons, just out-bid the scrappers. His plan was to refit the liner (and heavily market her glorious past history) as a combination cruise ship and floating university. She was registered in the Bahamas and renamed *Seawise University* ('Seawise' being a play on the owner's initials 'CY'). The liner limped to Hong Kong, a long, tedious voyage of breakdowns, boiler problems and a two-month wait at Aruba for emergency repairs.

The Tung interests spent $6 million on the ship at an anchorage in Hong Kong harbour, in a process of ferries filled with work crews and barges with machinery and parts quite similar to the liner's 1946 refit at the Tail of the Bank in Scotland. She was to be dry-docked in Japan at the conclusion of the refit. As always with the Queens, there was that nagging problem of adequate dry dock space. Even in as late as 1971, few shipyards in the world could handle them.

The operations of the *Seawise University*, again billed as the world's largest liner, were assigned to the Orient Overseas Line, a C. Y. Tung subsidiary and one already engaged in passenger ship services. The maiden cruise was advertised as 'the rebirth of a legend', and was to begin on 24 April 1972, a 75-day Circle Pacific cruise that was to sail from Los Angeles for Honolulu, Suva, Sydney, Fremantle, Bali, Singapore, Hong Kong, Kobe, Yokohama, Honolulu, Vancouver and return. *Per diem* rates were advertised for as little as $30 per day, a figure far less than Cunard could comparably offer in the new *QE2* at the time. Of course, operationally she would now cost far less, prompted mostly by the 1,200 or so all-Chinese crewmembers. Furthermore, it was planned that the former Cunarder would revisit New York, for the first time in over four years, as part of a world cruise at the end of the year, in December. Amidst such glorious plans was a tragic ending for the old Queen.

On the very eve of her departure for a Japanese shipyard, the *Seawise University* caught fire at Hong Kong on a Sunday afternoon, 9 January 1972. Similar to the demise of the *Normandie* exactly thirty years before, the fire spread rapidly throughout the ship as fireboats and tugs poured tons of water on the fiery, smokey hulk. She endured twenty-four hours of fire and explosion and then, as a Hong Kong Marine Department official described her end, 'She rolled over and died'. Again, the ex-Queen was in newspapers throughout the world. A smouldering wreck, she was half-sunk on her starboard side, the funnels canted over at an angle of 65°, her remains lying in 43 feet of water.

At the time of the fire, there was a party being held onboard for the conversion workers and their families. Of the 800–900 who were aboard, most of them left through safety exits, escaping onto nearby tugs and harbour craft. Another 200 workers jumped into the harbour waters before being rescued. Some clambered down ropes or the mammoth anchor chains. Only nine of those onboard were injured and, quite amazingly, there were no fatalities.

Arson was never ruled out as the cause of the fire. Primarily, the fires spread far too quickly. A Hong Kong fire official was quoted on the rapid spread of the fire as 'surprisingly, phenomenally fast'.

Months later, during the autumn of 1972, the *Miami Herald*

described the remains of the former *Elizabeth* as 'a fire-blackened corpse racked grotesquely by death throes and turned a dull red by rust. Her bridge has collapsed in on itself like a huge concertina and the big funnels lean at a sharp angle from the partly submerged wreck. The interior of the largest liner ever built is an unrecognizable mess of tangled steel.'

The gutted liner was beyond repair, of course, and given over to a Japanese salvage firm for scrapping on the spot. A boom surrounded her, trapping small amounts of escaping oil. Launches scurried back and forth, spraying emulsion on the oil to destroy it and to prevent any pollution threat to the harbour. Between August and October 1972, over 3,000 tons of oil trapped in the underwater tanks were pumped out into barges. Huge brackets were welded along the exposed port side, creating a workmen's walkway. From this foot-way, workers climbed on ladders to the top of the crumbled hull and superstructure. Rust was everywhere. The side of the ship, made of 2-in thick steel plating, had caved inwards and the steel decks had folded 'like cardboard'. Several hundred feet around the second, aft funnel was a gaping hole that disappeared into the oil-smeared waters. Through the portholes on the former A and B decks were pale green drops of a strange liquid. These were the remains of the melted brass fittings. Pieces of porthole glass had melted and then recrystallised, embedded with charcoal and extremely brittle.

By 1974, the wreck of the former *Queen Elizabeth* was gone. It was, indeed, a most pathetic ending to the second of the great Queens. Two bow letters — 'Q' and 'E' — were brought to New York and fitted into a memorial to the ship placed on the pavement just in front of the C. Y. Tung Building on Water Street.

The *Elizabeth* has been only a memory in recent years — in photographs, books, mementoes and models. Her life, which began so mysteriously with her secret passage to New York, ended so tragically. The *Mary* arrived in glory and remains with a sense of purpose to this day. It is to be hoped that she will endure for decades, a living monument to the great age of the ocean liner and to the most successful and popular pair of superliners ever built.

6

A New Ship, a New Crisis

On Friday, 19 March 1982, scientists of the British Antarctic Survey reported that a group of Argentinian scrap-metal salvagers had landed at the deserted whaling station at Leith, South Georgia, in the Southern Atlantic. Rather boldly, the 'salvagers' had raised the Argentinian flag over this small, rugged, British-held island, seemingly claiming it as their country's possession. At dawn, on 2 April, the Argentinian Army invaded the Falkland Islands and the scene was set for following weeks of tension, as Britain negotiated with an unyielding Argentina, and then high drama when the worst happened and an undeclared war was fought over the islands' bleak hills.

On Good Friday, 9 April, the P & O liner *Canberra*, requisitioned as a troopship to carry three of the five battalions making up 3 Commando Brigade (for the purposes of the Task Force this now consisted of the Royal Marines' 40, 42 and 45 Commandos along with the 2nd and 3rd Battalions of the Parachute Regiment and various support elements) and hurriedly fitted with helicopter flight decks, sailed to join the British Task Force that had left England on 5 April. Leaving bands playing among crowds of well-wishers on the quayside, the *Canberra* sailed from Southampton at dusk and, passing down a chilly Southampton Water, she was saluted by hundreds on the shoreline, shouting and flashing the headlights of their cars. It was the belief of many that a political solution would be found before the men on board the liner were needed.

From 25 April Cunard's *Queen Elizabeth 2* had been on a three-day visit to Philadelphia, her first, on a cruise to open the city's celebrations of the 200th anniversary of its founding. Thousands of visitors had been entertained and fed on board whilst she was there and goodwill to Britain was riding high. She sailed not knowing where her immediate future lay — would she carry on with her programme of cruises, advertised in a £½ million campaign or would she, too, be called up?

Feeling that some kind of service was on the cards, Phil Rentall, the *QE2*'s first officer, amused himself by doing a few hypothetical sums: 8,000 miles at 27.5 knots, an economical speed, would take around 10½ days, given good weather, 6,000 tonnes of fuel . . . Captain Hutcheson joked at Phil Rentall's efforts but was glad to have the information a few days later when questioned by the press.

At 12.30pm on 3 May, an hour after passing Bishop's Rock *en route* to Southampton, an announcement on BBC Radio told incredulous listeners that the *QE2* had indeed been requisitioned as a troopship. The BBC then telephoned Captain Hutcheson and asked if he had any further information, to which he could only answer 'No', as it was the first definite news that he had received. Some felt that it was a pity Cunard had not got in first with the information so that the captain could have been the one to break the news to the crew. The captain later made an announcement over the ship's broadcast system and confirmed to the ship's company what they perhaps by now already knew, but his announcement brought forth cheers.

The liner had seldom been out of the news throughout her entire career and, occasionally, had been faced with the threat of violence. The decision to build her at all was a battle in itself but this was against finance and traditional market concepts. The choice of a liner that would be built to combine regular passenger ferrying with cruising as a major revenue earner was an almost revolutionary concept. Her unfulfilled predecessor, known simply as Q3, was to have been a direct successor to the *Queen Mary* and *Queen Elizabeth*, but this type of passenger liner would have been outmoded by the mid-1960s for when she was planned. A radical change in philosophy by Cunard management brought forth a new ship project, known as Q4, which was to materialise in the brilliant and versatile *Queen Elizabeth 2*. The launching of the Q4, the second ship to bear the name 'Queen Elizabeth', took place on 20 September 1967, the christening being performed by Her Majesty Queen Elizabeth II.

Even when the liner was completed, her battle to survive was not over. Serious turbine troubles on trials delayed her maiden voyage by months and Cunard refused to accept her, at one time even considering selling her. After an enormous national publicity campaign that had built up anticipation of great success, the ship's engine trouble brought with it a lot of bad feeling with questions even being asked in Parliament. But once the problems were overcome the *QE2* became the glory of Britain's Mercantile Marine as she was intended to be and the past difficulties were forgotten.

Launched into a diminishing market as far as passenger ferrying was concerned, but also into the growing industry of cruising, her dual-purpose role was soon proven. She could voyage to places previously inaccessible to the *Mary* and *Elizabeth*, restricted by their breadths and draughts. The *QE2*'s designers made sure that she could traverse the Panama and Suez Canals and they also made sure she could use the hitherto inaccessible ports by reducing weight. Thus, from her very beginnings, both good and bad publicity kept her in the public eye and since her predecessors had disappeared into nostalgic history her very existence gave her an attraction and lustre equalling that of her forebears — except that she was yet to be proven in war. But drama, it seemed, was never far away.

In 1972, a Miss Shalvey, an evening-class pupil in New York, wrote a fictional essay basing the action on the *QE2*. Two of her characters, one terminally ill with cancer and the other an ex-convict as her accomplice, booked passage on the liner. Their plan was to hijack the ship and commit a daring jewel robbery (a real £26,000 jewel theft occurred on board, later, in 1978) or else blow up the ship with concealed devices. The story was read to the rest of the class.

On 17 May, shortly after the essay was read, a phone call was received at Cunard's New York office demanding a $350,000 ransom or else, said the caller, two passenger accomplices would detonate explosive devices concealed about the ship. Cunard collected the ransom money together and delivered it to the agreed pick-up point, but collection was never effected. Although a hoax was suspected the company was not prepared to take chances and the British authorities were alerted.

Whilst the *QE2* was homeward bound and almost 1,000 miles from Britain, two aircraft, a Hercules with bomb-disposal personnel on board and an accompanying Nimrod, being used for communications, circled around the liner which slowly came to a stop in mid-ocean. Figures dropped from the Hercules and as their parachutes opened on their descent a motor-launch, skippered by Junior First Officer R. A. Woodall, was lowered from the *QE2* into the sea. The weather, murky and misty with a Force 4 wind activating the water into a long swell, seemed to reflect the tense mood of the passengers as they watched, lining the ship's rails. The parachutists, as they landed in the sea ahead of the liner and just off her starboard bow, were soon picked up by the launch. In all, four men were dropped and they included representatives from the SAS (Special Air Service) and the SBS (Special Boat Squadron — the Royal Marines' equivalent of the SAS). Their leader, Captain Robert Williams, was led straight to the bridge where, with true British phlegm, he pulled from inside his wet-suit a daily newspaper which he presented to the ship's astonished captain.

Only a partial search of the huge liner was possible, with special attention being paid to the baggage storage areas, but nothing was found. Rumours, however, spread around the shipborne community. 'They've found two bombs already!' a stewardess excitedly announced to a crewmate.

As a sequel to the drama at sea, the evening-class professor, worried about the similarities of his pupil's fictional story and the realities of the *QE2* incident, telephoned the police, with the result that a New York shoe-salesman, Joseph Lindisi, was arrested and gaoled for twenty years, pending psychiatric reports, for perpetrating the hoax.

Groundings, minor collisions, the rescue of passengers from a burning liner in the Caribbean in 1971, an engine breakdown (caused by water and oil pipes being wrongly interconnected) when 1,564 passengers, the largest number to do so, were transferred to the *Sea Venture* 270 miles south west of Bermuda and fires including a serious, but successfully controlled, engine-room fire in 1976, maintained the *QE2* as a newsworthy item. But in 1973 an occurrence took place that could have seriously damaged the ship.

In 1974, whilst being interviewed on the BBC television programme *Panorama*, President Sadat of Egypt made a startling revelation. Egypt had, at that time, been sharing a political and military pact with Libya and one night in April 1973 President Sadat was awoken by a telephone call. A Soviet-built Egyptian submarine, based in Tripoli, had sailed on orders from Libya's leader, Colonel Qaddafi, and the submarine's commander wanted confirmation that he was to sink the *QE2*, at that time in the Mediterranean *en route* to Israel! Quickly overcoming the shock of the request, President Sadat rescinded his ally's order and told the commander to return his submarine to Alexandria, thus averting a disaster of international proportions.

The Israeli cruise, during which this event took place, was a charter trip organised by Oscar Rudnick of Assured Travel of Worcester, Massachusetts. He thought that many American and European Jews would like to cruise to Israel to join in the State's celebrations of the 25th anniversary of its foundation. Financial misunderstandings dogged the charter, with Cunard expecting the 1,200 passengers booked to travel in both directions. But the charterer intended the numbers to be a total carried during the whole cruise and consequently the liner was underbooked. Arab–Israeli tension was high and this was reflected in the liner's trip from New York to Southampton where she was promptly cordonned off. Divers made frequent inspections of the hull and police carefully studied passes of all those who had to go on board. Lorries were searched in the vicinity of the ship and the media had a field day. Crew members who had volunteered for the cruise were paid a bonus along with a promised four years' salary as compensation to their families should anything happen to them.

The *QE2* sailed on 16 April with crowds of spectators watching her departure from the shore, the mere suspicion of danger and excitement arousing public interest. During the voyage the reports emanating from the media angered many of the crew as being pure fabrication — if there was no real excitement then the journalists invented it. Whilst the liner was passing through the Strait of Gibraltar a live broadcast stated that several naval ships, including two large warships, could be seen leaving Gibraltar in the sunshine to take up line ahead and astern of the liner as she entered the Mediterranean. The liner's radio operator, listening to the broadcast, went out on deck but could see nothing of any naval ships in the prevailing gloomy conditions, let alone Gibraltar!

A black-out was operated on board during the last 100 miles of the trip through the Mediterranean but still the passengers enjoyed themselves, the food and entertainment, apparently oblivious of Qaddafi's nefarious plan. Security was tight but not apparent. Thirty Royal Marines and SAS men guarded the bridge and other key points but off duty kept themselves to themselves.

Sirens greeting her, the *QE2* arrived in Ashod, the largest ship to do so, on 21 April (a Saturday, which angered many orthodox Jews) and she was to stay there for five days. David Ben Gurion visited the ship on the Sunday; she then sailed for Haifa and ten days later returned to her first port of call. Motor torpedo boats patrolled the harbour's mouth and divers once again went down around the ship. At night the liner was floodlit and small anti-personnel charges were detonated in the surrounding water to deter aggressive divers. Crew-members, subject to the prevailing security screen, had to show their passes on leaving and entering both the ship and the dock area.

To help recoup his losses the charterer had planned to use the *QE2* as an hotel for guests, other than *bona fide* passengers, whilst the ship was in Israel but this was forbidden by the authorities on security grounds. At the completion of the cruise a ship full of happy passengers returned to Southampton on Sunday, 13 May, then New York, and more news coverage. Luckily unscathed, she was not without experience gained from the security exercises against the lurking dangers of terrorism.

The *QE2* also received unwanted custom from the IRA. In December 1974 an Irishman, Gabriel Megahey, a one-time Cunard employee, was arrested at his home in Southampton for being an arms negotiator for the IRA and subsequently he was deported to Belfast. The search that led to Megahey's arrest had started in 1971 when he had arranged for a veritable small arsenal to be shipped from New York to Cobh via the *QE2*. The blue and green suitcases in which the arms were concealed were unshipped on to the quayside of the Irish port and there, for one reason or another, they were left. It was only after the liner had sailed that a burly Irish stevedore saw them, tried to lift them, found that they were too heavy and alerted the Customs, and the arms were discovered. A supply of guns, ammunition and grenades was thus denied the terrorists and the resulting investigations traced a line to Megahey and his accomplices.

In spite of the *QE2*'s unsolicited forays into the realms of danger she has always been a popular ship with thousands of devoted followers, both in her cruising and Atlantic ferry roles. The rich and the famous, preferring the slower and more comfortable passage in an ocean liner to the rigours of jet-lag, often adorn the liner's passenger lists and help to maintain a part of the glamour that her predecessors had taken for granted. To cater for the ever-changing tastes of the travelling and cruising public the *QE2* has also proved to be very adaptable. Her internal layout has altered dramatically since she entered service. Carefully designed and decorated rooms have been swept away and replaced by more modern amenities. Today only two of her original public rooms remain — the Double Room (a two-tiered lounge), and the classically stylish Queen's Room, still modern and graceful after fifteen years of service. Even her external profile has been altered, with the addition in 1972 of pre-fabricated luxury penthouses abaft the bridge making her look rather more bulky and taller than she originally appeared.

But in May 1982 the *QE2* was on her way to her greatest trial. The liner docked in Southampton at two minutes past midnight on 4 May. News reporters and cameramen came down the next morning to interview crew and passengers. 'I hope they go get the bastards,' an obviously pro-British American stated as he disembarked. That same day HMS *Sheffield* was fatally hit by an Exocet missile, which more than underlined the need for troops in the South Atlantic.

The *QE2* was at war. Captain Peter Jackson, due to retire within a few months, took over the ship from Captain Hutcheson. Captain Jackson's responsibility would, however, extend only to the safety and navigation of his ship; her destination and orders lay in the hands of the Royal Navy. Captain James of the Royal Navy was to tell Captain Jackson: 'We will tell you what we want and you can do it.'

Over the next eight days, workmen from Vosper Thornycroft Shiprepairers in Southampton cut, burned, welded and fitted her out in military uniform, but even this could not blank out the luxury of the surroundings in which thousands of troops would travel to the war zone. Faces fell as a group of ship's officers was told by a Royal Navy representative where their beloved ship was to be mutilated to facilitate the fitting out of the after heli-pad. Several hundred feet of verandah windows would be cut away on two after decks and it was even suggested that the swimming-pools would be filled with cement to provide a base for the heli-pad and deck supports. In the event, the steel stanchions rested on protective pads laid on the pool bases and so a lot of top weight was eliminated. Underdeck supports for the heli-pads had also been erected in passenger cabins thus rendering them untenable for the duration of the voyage. Vospers had started to build the heli-pads prior to the *QE2*'s arrival and, when she had been prepared, the pads were lifted on to her by a floating crane and welded and bolted into place.

Thousands of square feet of hardboard were taped together to protect the remaining carpets in lounges and passageways against the forthcoming weeks of hard wear from military boots. The double lounge was converted into a dining room and the casino became a dormitory. Potted plants, paintings, pounds of caviar and the stock from the shopping arcade were amongst hundreds of items taken ashore for safe storage.

Crewmembers were given a choice — to sail with the liner, which would be carrying the 5th Infantry Brigade (see Appendix for the full list of units), or to stay at home on leave. Not many chose the latter course but those not needed immediately went on leave before parting from their families for an undetermined period. The stewards were released from duty altogether as 5 Brigade would provide its own messing arrangements. Crewmembers under eighteen years of age needed their parents' consent.

Ship's stores and military supplies arrived by the lorry-load — including 3 million Mars Bars to sustain the men in the field. Stores for three months were taken on board in nine days. As in preparations for the controversial Israeli cruise of 1973, police guarded entrances to the quay approaches and scrutinised passes carefully as people went on board.

A nineteen-year-old cook, Bob Bantock, watched the activity with interest, noting the extra effort the shipyard workers were making in order to get the liner ready on time. One of the few crewmen to be interested in the ship herself, not just regarding her as a means of livelihood, Bob wandered all over the ship fascinated by the preparations for war. Originally he had opted out of the voyage to the South Atlantic when volunteers were called for, to the great relief of his mother at home in Brighton. Later, after meeting a young friend who had just joined the Scots Guards and who would be going south on the *QE2*, Bob quickly changed his mind. It took him a little while to get Cunard to change their minds too, but his eagerness got him a post as a night baker. Working nights enabled him to observe the conversion work and later troop-training during the day.

Motorways and lanes in and around Hampshire became busy as the green-painted trucks of the 5th Infantry Brigade converged on Southampton Docks. Some people may have felt that the government was using the *QE2* — the flagship of Britain's Merchant Marine — as a grand but extravagant gesture, but this was not so. Three thousand men in one brigade were needed quickly in the South Atlantic to back up the men already on their way there in the *Canberra* and the other ships of the Task Force, and the *QE2* was the only ship that could do it. The Merchant Marine was once again proving its worth after nearly twenty years of neglect. Unromantically, the merchant ships used in the Falklands crisis became known, in true abbreviated military style, as 'STUFT' (Ships Taken Up From Trade).

The dock workers in Southampton found that the cargo they were loading differed from their usual fare. From 9 May metal boxes of ammunition went aboard by the hundred. These boxes, once emptied after small-arms practice on the way south, made useful tool boxes and were eagerly sought after by the crew.

By the second week of May the *QE2* was almost ready, although a definite sailing date had not been announced. The forward and after

122

heli-pads were almost complete but left as bare steel to be painted en voyage. Other parts of the ship that had been cut away were also left bare, and if they were not painted during the voyage then they would return rusty. Several important naval fittings were installed to assist in communications and in the protection of the ship. For the former, small conical UHF aerials were fitted on both bridge wings and white SCOT (Satellite Communications Onboard Tracker) domes shaped like hot-air balloons, were installed with their temporary cabins aft of the luxury penthouse suites on the uppermost deck. To reduce the natural magnetic field of the liner and to help protect her from influencing magnetic mines, a degaussing cable was fitted inside the ship and a low current of electricity was passed through the coil. Similar coils had been fitted to the *Queen Mary* and *Queen Elizabeth* during World War II and had been housed in the continuous fore and aft bulges that could be seen on the outside of their hulls along the sheer line. Guns, too, would help protect the *QE2* from attack but these would be fitted onto seatings constructed during the voyage.

Accommodation was sorted out and a list showing where troop units were to be billeted was posted on the notice board. First Officer Rentall had gone on leave to get his uniform of a lieutenant in the Royal Naval Reserve, having been appointed liaison officer between the ship and the naval staff on board. His new boss was to be Captain Noel 'Jimmy' James, the Royal Naval captain in overall charge of the liner and, as liaison officer, Phil Rentall managed to secure one of the luxury penthouses on the liner's top deck, with an adjoining companionway to Captain James's quarters.

During the afternoon of 11 May, troop preparation parties arrived on board and just before 6am the next morning the first of the troops belonging to 5 Brigade, the 1st Battalion the Welsh Guards, arrived at the quayside and clambered quickly on board.

Since the early hours, sweethearts, wives, relatives, friends and the curious had waited outside the dock gates in Canute Road hoping to catch a glimpse of someone they knew amongst the troops as they arrived. The various units that were to make up the Brigade arrived on board at quarter-hourly intervals and were hastily led to their quarters. At 10am the 1st Battalion, the 7th Duke of Edinburgh's Own Gurkha Rifles arrived amidst great excitement, their backpacks almost as big and heavy as their bearers. The Gurkhas were to be berthed low down in the ship on 5 Deck. Fearsome soldiers though the Gurkhas were, they were notoriously bad sailors and it was felt that they would be less prone to seasickness where the movement of the ship was least. The last of the troops embarked at 11am.

Over years of warfare it had been realised that an artist can capture more of the feel of a campaign than can be conveyed by words or a camera, so also embarking that day was Linda Kitson, commissioned by the Imperial War Museum and the Fleet Air Arm Museum as their accredited official War Artist. She started drawing almost immediately after her arrival.

The day of sailing — Wednesday 12 May — dawned bright and clear with Southampton Water looking its springtime best. The dockside gradually filled with the first of the many thousands who would eventually come to cheer the liner away. Lord Matthews, chairman of Trafalgar House, the parent company of the Cunard line, and John Nott, the British Defence Secretary, accompanied by Ian McDonald, the Ministry of Defence spokesman made famous by his 'matter-of-fact' television bulletins, arrived and spent some time on board. John Nott moved swiftly amongst the troops so as to avoid any searching questions. The area to the north of the Queen Elizabeth II passenger terminal, normally reserved for the mass parking of imported cars, took on the look of a mini heli-port as the VIP visitors arrived and departed.

A Lynx helicopter on the *QE2*'s after heli-pad. The pads required daily maintenance and, each evening after flying operations were over for the day, painting squads repainted the pads with anti-slip paint and freshened-up the landing markings (*Wally Adams*)

In one of the *QE2*'s lounges troops practise with automatic weapons. Blindfolds were worn to accustom the men in dismantling and assembling weapons in darkness. War does not always wait for daylight! (*Imperial War Museum*)

An extemporised swimming pool on the *QE2*'s forward heli-pad became the boisterous scene of the 'crossing the line' ceremony (*Imperial War Museum*)

By mid-afternoon 3,000 faces strove to look down from the liner at the people gathering on the quayside who, in turn, looked up at the ship hoping to catch a glimpse of a loved one in the crowd. Flags and home-made banners, some bearing regimental names and some personal messages, were hung over the ship's side and similar banners were held up high from the quay. The topless wife of one of the embarked troops waved her discarded bra to her husband before allowing a dockside crane to lift it carefully on board to him. A scantily clad young lady delivered a singing telegram to her soldier brother, much to the delight of his 'oppos'. Excitement grew as 4pm approached. A military band played lustily as tears, shouts and waves were exchanged between the ship and shore. A bevy of tugs busied themselves catching and securing lines thrown from the ship which would pull her away from the quay and into Southampton Water. The ship still flew the Red Ensign as, although she carried naval personnel, she was regarded as an unprotected merchant ship.

Meanwhile, activity of another kind was happening deep down inside the liner's boiler room. Of the three boilers, two were out of action and the one remaining operational would not, by itself, get the *QE2* very far. Two boilers, at least, were needed to supply the ship with enough power to provide lighting, pumping facilities and, most importantly, power for propelling the ship at an adequate speed to maintain safe manoeuvrability. Two boilers had been serviceable on the previous day, having undergone refits, but a massive leakage had been discovered in the essential distilled-feed-water system. The faulty boiler was hurriedly closed down, the third boiler was just completing its refit, and immediate investigations began to find the

Cross-decking took place via trawlers, an admiralty tug and the *QE2*'s own boats. Weather conditions changed rapidly with fog, sleet, snow and clear spells following each other as winter in the southern hemisphere started to make itself felt (*Imperial War Museum*)

British troops cross-decking in misty conditions via one of the *Ella* trawlers as she backs away from the *QE2* in Cumberland Bay, South Georgia. These trawlers, requisitioned as minesweepers, shuttled between the *QE2* and the *Canberra* and *Norland*, carrying both troops and stores (*Imperial War Museum*) cause of the trouble. It was thought at first that perhaps leaky water tubes were to blame and as the leakage was exceeding the distilled-water production of the ship's plant, the fault had to be found quickly.

. But, in spite of these worries which were of great concern to those few who were aware of them, the ship was expected to sail and so sail she must. Amidst the noise and excitement on the quayside, the ship's siren booming above all else, the *QE2* slipped her moorings a few minutes after 4pm and was pulled, slowly at first, away from her berth — the gap between her and the quay gradually widening.

With the band now playing 'Auld Lang Syne' the *QE2*, with her bow still pointing upstream, loomed over the tugs that were gently but powerfully coercing her into movement. When she reached a point just off the disused Ocean Terminal she was swung around through a full circle until she was pointing downstream towards the Isle of Wight. After a while the tugs *Calshot* and *Clausentum* let go of the forward lines and the *Romsey* and *Brockenhurst* let go aft leaving just one tug, the *Albert*, pulling at a solitary forward line. By now the troops had traversed the decks to the port side of the liner and crowded every vantage point, even climbing into the lifeboats and up the cargo cranes, to wave and cheer goodbye. The strains of a lone piper drifted across the water from the liner to the spectators on the shore.

A strong wind was blowing and because the *QE2* had insufficient power to manoeuvre properly by herself the little *Albert* had to guide her all the way down Southampton Water at the slow pace of 6 knots. As she manoeuvred around the reversed 'S' bend channel between Calshot Spit and Cowes the cheering crowds lining the surrounding shores were unaware that the liner was, in effect, crippled. Just before 6pm the *Albert* let go her line and the *QE2* was on her own. Two Sea King helicopters circled her, feeling the turbulence caused by her slow forward movement, before making two perfect landings, the first of many to follow.

As the last of the spectators wended their way homeward, the *QE2*, leaving the Nab Tower 3 miles astern, was brought to a stop in decreased visibility that rendered her invisible from the shore and anchored in the Channel just before 8.30. She was unable to proceed any further until the troublesome leak had been traced and stopped. Fortunately, perhaps, the press was not on hand to witness this unfortunate and potentially embarrassing delay. The ship prepared for an overnight stay where she lay whilst her engineers frantically searched for the cause of the trouble and tried to get a second boiler, at least, into operation. With a real feeling of relief the fault was finally traced; a valve had simply been left open and the few turns it took to close it brought the boiler, and with it the ship, back into business. Taking advantage of this unscheduled and unpublicised stay in the approaches to Spithead, the Admiralty tug *Bustler*, out of Portsmouth, brought out last-minute stores.

At 9.30am on Thursday, 13 May, a fine but cloud–scattered day with a choppy sea, the anchor was weighed and soon the *QE2* was making her maximum speed obtainable on two boilers. The 3,900 people on board were now truly on their way to a destination as yet unknown. An hour later the troops were put through their first lifeboat drill. With more passengers to a cabin than usual and with extra men berthed in improvised dormitories, the lifeboat stations became impossibly overcrowded but, from the confusion, a practical lifeboat drill evolved utilising plans for the extra inflatable liferafts that were being carried. Another drill would be held the next day, others would follow, using the revised plans.

The *QE2* headed westward down the choppy Channel, which was undulating with a slight swell. In the early evening of this first complete day out a helicopter was made ready to fly off the ship with a soldier suffering from suspected appendicitis, accompanied by two of the liner's medical staff, who were quite excited at the prospect of a flight from their ship. Their destination was Trelisk Hospital in Cornwall and when the helicopter returned to the ship two hours later its passengers and crew brought with them welcome newspapers gleaned by various means from both patients and staff at the hospital.

'Stand by Engines' was rung just after 6pm and the *QE2*'s speed was reduced from 21 knots to 13 knots. She was to rendezvous with the Royal Fleet Auxiliary ship *Grey Rover* to try the difficult manoeuvre of refuelling at sea whilst underway — an exercise known to the Royal Navy as 'Replenishment at Sea' or 'rassing'. The Navy had developed and perfected this practice over many years, overcoming the problems of interaction between two or more vessels sailing in close proximity. The Russians, who have evidently not yet mastered this feat, showed great interest in the operation whenever one of their profusely aerialled 'trawlers' — auxiliary intelligence-gathering vessels (AIGs) — drew within range. Rassing had only recently been tried with merchant ships but the mercantile marine soon picked up the method under the expert guidance of the RFA.

It was now the turn of the *QE2* to make her rassing debut. The *Grey Rover*, a small Fleet tanker and store ship, approached carefully from astern and, reducing speed to take up her position alongside the liner's starboard side, shot a line across to which was attached an 8-in fuel hose. A hundred soldiers hauled on the line until the hose appeared through the baggage port on 2 Deck where the ship's coupling point had been fitted with piping leading down to the fuel tanks. Connections were made and a few tonnes were transferred during a minute's pumping. The hose was then blown through to clear it, disconnected and returned to the *Grey Rover*. At 7.30 the *QE2* resumed her speed and course; the whole operation, which had lasted just over an hour, had been a great success. Relief was felt that the liner would not be without a supply of fuel whenever or wherever it was needed.

Dusk fell and at 10pm the *QE2* altered course towards the Bay of Biscay, steaming along at 23 knots, her destination now known to be Freetown in Sierra Leone. Three thousand miles of ocean still lay between her and the port and she endeavoured to keep away from the regular shipping routes. The eventful first day at sea came to a successful conclusion when, at around midnight, the third boiler was brought into operation and maximum speed was again made available.

The following day the ship's company knuckled down to a routine that it would follow over the ensuing days. One of the first priorities was to practise lifeboat and raft drill using the newly evolved plans, and the ship's officers, with the help of Regimental Sergeant Major

Hunt, sorted out the men until an efficient order of evacuation had been planned. The Gurkhas sat patiently and cross-legged at their stations; these soldiers, berthed low down in the ship, had been trained to find their way to their boat-stations in the dark should the ship's power fail. Blindfolded they would find their way up through the ship, groping along corridors. It was not uncommon for a Gurkha to lose his way and be seen staggering and bumping against chairs and tables in a restaurant; the witnesses to such events were amused but impressed by such determination.

The troops also organised their training schedules, each company having its own specific time for using the swimming-pool or for jogging, full-packed, around the deck, and these times were jealously guarded. The Gurkhas were first on deck at 6am — these diminutive soldiers dwarfed by their British officers. Bob Bantock, the young night baker, also enjoyed an early jog, albeit in a more leisurely fashion. Thinking that no harm would be done if he was on deck very early in the morning, he was soon disillusioned when he was brusquely pushed to one side by a 6ft-plus officer of the Gurkhas who snapped 'Get off the deck! This is our time!'

From mid-morning small-arms practice was scheduled, the firing ranges being the heli-pads. A careful watch was kept for other ships in case any came within range. The *QE2* did not want a reputation for being trigger-happy! Off-duty crewmembers found that the staccato chorus from the upper decks made rest difficult. It was during one of these practices that the *QE2* received her 'war-wound'. Blazing away with an automatic weapon on the forward flight deck, a gunner caught one of the vertical, tubular stanchions that made up part of the guardrails and a small hole neatly pierced it through. This same hole is still kept — unrepaired — a lasting souvenir of a self-inflicted injury. Some of the rubbish bags that were normally discharged at night to help cover the passing of the liner, were sometimes used as targets and sunk. When small-arms practice was finished for the day, spent cartridge cases littered the deck like so many discarded cigarette ends.

On Saturday, 15 May, units of the SAS landed on Pebble Island off the north-western coast of West Falkland, destroying eleven

Argentinian aircraft before withdrawing. Things were hotting up with the political situation becoming even more of an impasse as politicians and diplomats journeyed back and forth in search of a peaceful solution. The answer to the problem seemed to be immediate implementation of Resolution 502 of the United Nations Security Council (the resolution demanded an immediate cessation of hostilities and an immediate withdrawal of all Argentinian forces from the Falkland Islands, and called on the Governments of Argentina and the United Kingdom to seek a diplomatic solution). However, the Argentines refused to quit the islands and were adamant that the 'Malvinas' belonged to them.

As the *QE2* made her way towards Africa the weather above the Equator was a mixture of spring and summer. The voyage almost had the feel of a cruise except that the passengers were not in a holiday mood, even if they did not yet know whether they would be needed in earnest. Just over five days after leaving Southampton the *Queen* was in the approaches to Freetown and two pilots climbed to the bridge from their cutter in order to assist in the navigation of the liner to her berth at the Queen Elizabeth II Quay. One of the pilots, immaculate in his white uniform and plethora of gold braid, caused a mild sensation on the bridge by sporting a thick-heeled pair of the brightest green shoes! The *QE2* had not been expected at the port and the pilots looked first at the ship, then at the quay where the liner was to be berthed and one said to the Captain 'I think you had better do it, Captain!' On the quayside cargo containers had been piled up to form security walls between dockside buildings.

By midday on 18 May the liner was moored, port side to the quay. She took on fresh water and 1,900 tonnes of fuel, pumped into her tanks from both shore and barge supplies. So far she had steamed nearly 3,000 miles at an average speed of 24.35 knots and had, at times, achieved 25.25 knots. No one, except the Cunard agent, was allowed ashore, although a rumour amongst the crew said that one of their number had gone ashore and that the ship had sailed without him. This rumour proved to be true. The crewman had somehow managed to slip ashore, evidently to purchase drugs, had not been able to get back on board, missed the ship and was subsequently sent home and dismissed. The Cunard Agent reported that the man had told him that he had fallen overboard, swum about outside the harbour for several hours before being picked up by a fishing boat and reporting to the Agent. An amazing feat of swimming considering that the waters in that area were infested with sharks!

A noisy, jostling, bartering fleet of local traders' boats bustled alongside the liner's hull. The usual tourist trinkets were offered for sale and the First Officer suspected that some of the ship's silver, amongst other things, disappeared over the side in exchange. Eventually the 'bum-boats' as they are popularly called, were ordered to leave as it was considered possible that the animal skins that were being offered for sale could be carriers of anthrax.

Eleven hours after her arrival the *QE2* left Freetown, which turned out to be the scene of her last docking until she returned to Southampton four weeks later.

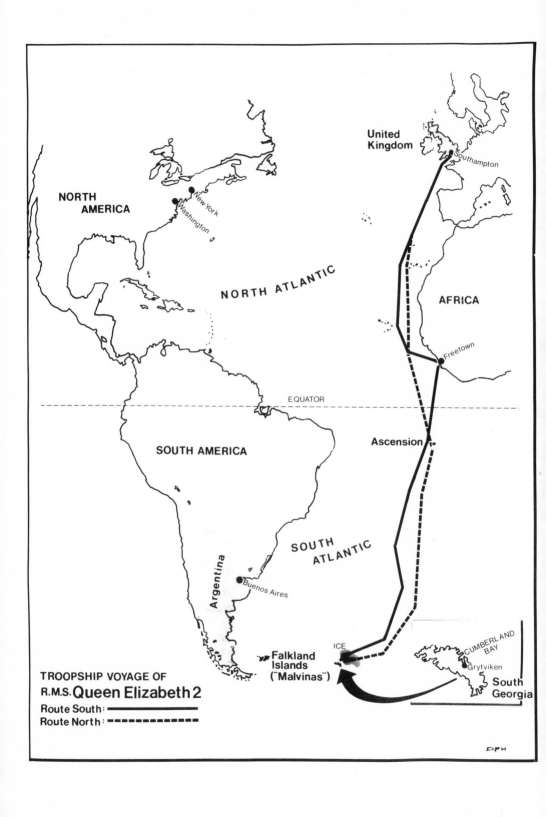

NORTH
AMERICA

New York
Washington

NORTH ATLANTIC

EQUATOR

SOUTH AMERICA

SOUTH
ATLANTIC

Argentina

Buenos Aires

Falkland
Islands
("Malvinas")

ICE

United
Kingdom

Southampton

AFRICA

Freetown

Ascension

CUMBERLAND
BAY

Grytviken

South
Georgia

TROOPSHIP VOYAGE OF
R.M.S. Queen Elizabeth 2
Route South :————
Route North :———————

DFH

7

The War Zone

By midnight on 18 May the Cape Sierra Leone light was well astern and the *QE2*'s telegraphs rang 'Full Ahead' and the engine revolutions crept up to 140rpm. Two hours later at a position of 8°N, 13°59W, the ship altered course by 182°. During her first day out of Freetown she steamed a distance of 594 nautical miles. She was now headed for Ascension Island, far out in the Atlantic.

Flying off the helicopters now became a daily routine. At this time it was essential that the troops were rehearsed in the methods of embarking, fully kitted, on to the helicopters as it was not yet known whether or not 5 Brigade would be disembarked by air or by sea. After each day's flying a squad would busy themselves on the flight deck repainting and repairing the pads ready for the next day's operations which would, in turn, obliterate the freshly painted markings and provide more work for the following evening.

Between Freetown and Ascension both Brigadier Tony Wilson, 5 Brigade's commanding officer, and Captain James gave lectures to the crew of the *QE2* showing slides of British and Argentinian ships that might be expected to be in the South Atlantic. Brigadier Wilson was obviously moved when he told the crew that he, and the troops, had great respect for them as they were the only ones on board to have volunteered to go south. Everybody else was there because they had to be, it was their job.

The *QE2* crossed the Equator during the night of 19–20 May and the troops were determined not to let the traditional event of 'Crossing the Line' pass without celebration. A wood-and-canvas swimming pool, constructed between the two forward cranes, became the scene of good-natured celebrations as pies were thrown, green and red dye foam splashed around and a vile-smelling liquid concocted by the troops assaulted the noses of the spectators as King Neptune initiated the first-time 'line crossers' in a messy ritual.

On Thursday morning, 20 May, a Russian AIG approached the ship for a good look before turning and sailing away. Later that day the *QE2* reduced speed to rendezvous with HMS *Dumbarton Castle*, a small naval vessel originally built for fisheries and oil-rig protection. Two helicopters transferred stores from the little grey craft, pitching slightly in the Atlantic swell, to the steady giant a few hundred yards away. The two ships made their farewells just after 4pm and the superliner steamed slowly along waiting until the next day when Major-General Jeremy Moore, commander of the land forces, and his staff would join the ship by helicopter after being flown out from the UK to Ascension that evening.

Black-out was now being vigorously imposed, with thousands of black plastic covers, cut from wooden templates, covering every window and porthole on the ship. Troops were made responsible for their own quarters, with special squads blacking-out the public rooms. The results were most effective and when the task was completed the ship could not be seen at night other than for her navigation lights. She had been converted, to quote Captain James, 'from the brightest star on the ocean to the darkest'. The Navy's own system of landing lights enabled the inspecting helicopter to land safely. The plastic black-out covers, although efficient in their purpose, also caused the temperature in the liner to soar uncomfortably whilst the *QE2* passed through the tropical zones.

Friday, 21 May, dawning cloudy but becoming fine and clear, was to be an important day both to the *QE2* and to the people of the Falkland Islands. In the late evening British troops landed at San Carlos to establish a bridgehead for the eventual retaking of the Falklands while they awaited the arrival of Major-General Moore. For the *QE2* and her complement it meant a busy day and from 8am helicopters flew back and forth from Ascension to the ship carrying stores and mail. The liner, continuously on the move for safety, kept changing course so as not to sail too far away from the island. The forward helipad was used on occasions, the pilot of the craft landing there having to remind himself that there were several thousand tons of steel-encased luxury coming towards him at 18 knots!

The most important items to be embarked during the day were Major-General Jeremy Moore and his staff, who were accommodated in the better type of cabin. Phil Rentall, the First Officer, had to move out of his single cabin to share the upper part of the two-storeyed Trafalgar Suite with two military officers. Two engine-room staff were flown off the ship to Ascension, one with a fracture and the other with a blood disease from which he later died.

The *QE2* was now part of a convoy, spread along a long path between the British Isles and the South Atlantic. A day ahead steamed the sister-ships *Nordic Ferry* and *Baltic Ferry* and behind was another Cunarder, the *Atlantic Causeway*. It was the *Causeway*'s ill-fated sister-ship the *Atlantic Conveyor* that was to be fatally hit by a missile on 25 May — an event that brought home, probably more than anything else, to fellow Cunard crewmembers on board *QE2* the gravity and danger of their mission.

Contact was made with the *Atlantic Causeway* in the early hours of 22 May, and by 7am helicopters were flying between the two ships, once again transferring stores. Leaving Ascension meant that all personnel on board were now on active duty and that the time had come to get down to business. The *QE2* was isolated from the rest of the world and with her radio and radar shut down the ship became electronically 'silent'. This was essential if missiles that homed in on radio transmissions were to be avoided, and the navigating officers had to rely on 'the Mark 1 eyeball'! Major-General Moore suffered more than anyone; held almost incommunicado, he could not send out messages to direct the campaign. But the men felt the pinch too, isolation also meant a lack of regular mail and the ability to send letters home. Linda Kitson, the war artist, noted a drop in morale. One source of incoming information was the BBC World Service news and reports were eagerly digested. Other information came through the naval SCOT system that had been installed aft of the luxury penthouses.

The *QE2* was also being armed. Blowpipe anti-aircraft missiles were installed around the base of the funnel; Browning automatic weapons were installed on specially built mountings on each bridge wing and aft by the shopping arcade. Two days before arrival at

South Georgia, they were noisily tested although one of the bridge weapons refused to work. Sentries, some armed, were maintained, the top of the funnel casing being used for this purpose on occasions.

Daily drill, weapon practice and helicopter embarkation kept the troops busy. A steady flow of troops and crewmembers studied the large-scale map of the Falklands that hung outside the Columbia Restaurant, where in more peaceful times hung tapestries of the building and launching of the liner. Charts showing profiles of both British and Argentinian ships were also studied and lists of losses sustained by both sides were kept up to date.

The troops kept themselves amused during their off-duty hours rehearsing and performing concert parties and producing a daily news sheet, quoting extracts from the BBC World Service. The men ate well too, the food including a wide choice of salads and plenty of fresh fruit. The Scots and Welsh Guards ate in the Columbia Restaurant, the Gurkhas in Tables of the World and the officers from the penthouse suites ate in the Queens Grill where they had waiter service. The Penthouse Grill became the Sergeants' and Petty Officers' Mess. At night the crewmen left tea and cocoa in the pantry so that the troops could make themselves a hot drink if they wished, and tea and sandwiches were always available for the helicopter crews. As the food stores carried were government issue, no unauthorised person was allowed in the galley and MPs were put on guard. One lad, however, was detained for attempted pilfering at 2am one morning.

At the outset of the voyage it was thought that fresh water would be in short supply but the ship's newly installed reverse osmosis system and four distilling plants produced more water than could be consumed. The Gurkhas, believing that the toilets were flushed with fresh and not salt water, had to be ordered to flush them in their eagerness to save water.

Belligerent submarines were always a threat but luckily the prime target of the Argentinians was left alone. It was suspected, however, that the Russians were tracking the liner with their satellites but, perhaps because their political ideals were opposed to those of Argentina, the *QE2*'s location was not passed on.

Steaming south at an average speed of 25.5 knots the *QE2* gradually sailed into colder weather as she neared the winter that was beginning in the southern hemisphere. Temperatures fell from the 28°C that had been experienced at noon-day off Ascension to 5°C five days later as the liner approached the iceberg zone. The weather, too, gradually deteriorated, becoming overcast and rainy. On 25 May, with changing winds, the sea left behind its low swell of the previous day to become moderate. To give the troops some additional comfort, since they were after all on board one of the luxury ships of all time, the stabilisers were brought into operation. Tragedy once again struck the Royal and Merchant Navies on this day when HMS *Coventry*, sister-ship to the *Sheffield*, was lost and the Cunard containership *Atlantic Conveyor* was abandoned after being hit by an Exocet missile. Destroyed with her were three essential Chinook heavy-lift helicopters.

From 3.30pm (which was near to dusk) on 26 May visibility was so reduced as to cause concern and it was therefore decided to take a chance with enemy missiles and switch the radar on once every 30 minutes. The captain was called and the engines put on to 'Stand By' as, highlighted on the radar screen with 'unnerving clarity', as First Officer Phil Rentall put it, at least 100 icebergs could be seen scattered about the region. That evening the watertight doors were closed with more earnestness than usual with the second enemy — ice — now lurking about in the surrounding ocean. Phil Rentall, perhaps one amongst others, remembered another night just over seventy years ago when the *Titanic* sank after grazing one of these mountains of ice that now drifted silently about the *QE2* in the dark. He prayed that history would not repeat itself. Speed was reduced to 9 knots. This would lead to a late rendezvous with *Antrim* but the captain said that it would be better to get there in one piece.

In the 26 May edition of *5th Infantry Brigade–QE2 News* Brigadier Wilson wrote the following message to all on board the liner:

Very shortly we shall all transfer to other ships off South Georgia and start on the last phase of our move to the Falkland Islands. It looks as if the Brigade will be there about 1st June, that is early next week.

Once there, we shall join 3 Commando Brigade. We shall sort ourselves out and then start joint operations to recapture the Islands.

Orders will be given out on landing; it is too early yet to issue a detailed plan, for it would be bound to change over the course of the next five days.

This is the final issue of this newspaper and to the Master and Ship's Company of *QE2* I would say 'Thank you' for the way you have looked after us on this voyage. We have come to know you well, we admire you, and we shall always be proud that we sailed with you in your magnificent ship.

To the Brigade I would simply say this: 'We shall start earning our pay as a team shortly — and we are in this game to win!'

Brigadier Wilson was later to back up his thanks by cruising on the *QE2* and giving the crew a greatly appreciated talk on what happened after 5 Brigade left their ship.

All through the early morning of 27 May the captain stayed on the bridge with the ship on 'Ice Routine'. The radar was switched on again briefly and engine revolutions were reduced to 80rpm. Variations in revolutions took place throughout the morning which, as it dawned, brought forth an awesome spectacle. Icebergs reflecting the rays of the early morning sun shone radiantly in all tones of red, yellow and orange. Phil Rentall calculated that one berg, looming up from its surrounding cushion of mist, must have been a mile long and 300ft high. As the *QE2* was guided safely away from it, this giant of a berg was enveloped by a blanket of mist leaving its outline barely discernible through the gloom.

The sea state had reduced to a long swell in the ice region and appeared to be unusually calm for the area considering the time of year. At 11.30am the liner came to a halt in the prevailing overcast and foggy conditions. The temperature was 3°C. A rendezvous was to be made with the County Class guided-missile destroyer HMS *Antrim* at a position of 52°43'S and 35°15'W and the naval ship quickly hove into view. The *QE2*'s officers expressed their admiration at the skill of the navigators of the *Antrim* in finding the rendezvous point so quickly and accurately. This admiration was crushed somewhat when the Royal Navy said that they had pinpointed the *QE2*'s position quite easily when the liner had switched on her radar for a short while whilst in the midst of the icefield!

The purpose of the rendezvous was to transfer Major-General Moore and his staff to the *Antrim*, battle-scarred and streaked with

140

rust, which would then take them on the next stage of their journey to the invasion base near San Carlos settlement on East Falkland. There the troops already ashore were eagerly awaiting his arrival so that they could proceed with their advance. The general and his senior staff were cross-decked by helicopter but the majority of his men were ferried across by the *QE2*'s motor launches. The long swell was deeper than at first thought and the troops had to jump on board the launches and again on to a rope ladder on boarding the *Antrim*, when their launch reached the crest of a wave. One junior officer took longer than he should in completing his climb up the ladder and as a consequence his leg was broken when it was caught between the *Antrim* and the rising launch. Lifted aboard the destroyer he was later returned to the *QE2* by helicopter. For him, at least, the war was over.

At 1.30pm the two ships parted company in the fog, the *Antrim* sailing towards the war zone and the *QE2*, retrieving her boats from the swell and damaging the davit bedplates in the process, to South Georgia, a destination that had not been revealed until three days previously. 'Stand by Engines' was rung on the telegraph at 5.45pm and twenty minutes later Right Whale Rocks on South Georgia were sighted. There was a depth of water in the bay of 360ft which was too deep to drop the anchor in one operation, the anchor and cables could not have been stopped and would have torn the securing shackles from the collision bulkhead. To prevent this happening the captain ordered 3 shackles (270ft) of cable to be paid out and suspended beneath the bow as the *QE2* approached her anchorage and to pay out the remaining 90ft of cable once the ship was in position. Just after 6.30 the starboard anchor, amidst a cloud of rust and sparks, was let go and splashed into the water, care being taken to use the anchor brake to prevent the complete length of cable from running wildly away. Meantime the ship went slowly astern in the calm waters of Cumberland Bay so as to lay the cable out along the sea bed; she was at rest for the first time in almost nine days since leaving Freetown, 5,035 nautical miles away. Supervising the task of anchoring, the first officer noticed that even with the lights on he could not see the liner's bridge from his position forward as the fog was still quite dense. By 7.30 anchoring was completed and the 963ft length of the *QE2* lay at rest a mile from Grytviken, site of a British Antarctic Survey base and a former whaling station. The engine-room was, however, put on immediate notice, the ship ready to bolt at the first sign of danger.

The troops were to go without a final night's sleep on the ship; it had been decided to start off-loading them immediately by sea, as it was so calm, and not by the much-exercised helicopter transference that would have been used had the weather been blustery. So, at 9.20pm, the STUFT trawler *Cordella* came alongside the *QE2*'s starboard side amidships and twenty-five minutes later the first of the troops started disembarking.

The majority of the disembarked troops were to be cross-decked to the P & O liner *Canberra* that had been anxiously awaiting the Cunarder's appearance since her own arrival earlier that afternoon. Red rust streaks running down her normally brilliant white sides the *Canberra* had been through a lot during the seven days since her arrival in San Carlos water in the early hours of 21 May. Air raids had started at dawn that day and by mid-afternoon the *Canberra* herself, straddled by bombs, witnessed the bombing and abandoning of HMS *Ardent*. The survivors of the frigate's crew were helped on board the liner two hours later and were well cared for over the following days by the liner's crew, many of whom felt sad to see them leave when they finally transferred to the *QE2*.

Also out in the fog and darkness of Cumberland Bay was the P & O ferry *Norland* of 13,000 tons. She had left Portsmouth on 26 April with 600 men of 2 Para and she, too, had seen action — a line of cannon holes bearing witness to her proximity to danger. Her complement had been credited with shooting down an Argentinian

Two of the trawler/minesweepers alongside the *QE2* in Cumberland Bay, South Georgia. The *Canberra* can be seen in the distance with the Admiralty tug *Typhoon* alongside (*Wally Adams*)

At 9.45am on Friday 11 June, 1982, the *QE2* sailed past the Royal Yacht *Britannia*. Her Majesty Queen Elizabeth The Queen Mother can be seen on the far (port) after side of the yacht's boat deck (*Southern Newspapers plc, Southampton*)

aircraft by putting up a 'wall of fire' from small arms and her deck had been showered with wreckage from a Skyhawk aircraft, destroyed by a land-fired Rapier missile. She brought with her for transfer to the *QE2*, survivors from *Ardent*'s sister-ship HMS *Antelope*. In return, *Norland* was destined to embark the Gurkhas on the final leg of their journey.

Transference of troops and stores continued through the night. A plan had been evolved to get the troops off as quickly as possible. If necessary, stores, ammunition and 400 troops could follow later in the RFA *Stromness* which would bring yet more survivors, this time from HMS *Coventry*.

The trawlers that were to be used as ferries between the Cunarder and the *Canberra* and *Norland* had been taken over by Royal Naval personnel, much to the chagrin of their peacetime fishermen crews who had wanted to 'have a go' themselves. They were the *Northella*, *Junella*, *Farnella* and *Cordella*, collectively known as the Ellas, all of between 1,200 to 1,500 tons and belonging to J. Marr & Son Ltd of Hull, and the *Pict* of British United Trawlers; all had been modified for use by the 11th Minesweeping Squadron. The Admiralty tug *Typhoon* was also being used and troops embarked on to these small but seaworthy ferries from the lower deck along the *QE2*'s sides.

Shortly after dawn the fog lifted slightly and the improved visibility brought with it a spectacle of natural grandeur; the high, ice-covered peaks of South Georgia, disappearing into the low clouds through which an occasional patch of blue sky could be seen, dwarfed the waiting ships. In the distance, yellowish columns of smoke angled up from the *Canberra*'s twin funnels before blending into the low cloud base. Another Cunard ship was also there, the *Saxonia*, a cargo ship that had brought stores from the UK to

Escorted by a flotilla of small craft, the *QE2* approaches Southampton. Survivors from the sunken warships can be seen lining the liner's heli-pads (*R. Bruce Grice*)

David Hart-Dyke, captain of the lost HMS *Coventry*, is welcomed home as he steps ashore. His facial injuries, caused by the flashes generated by the explosion when his ship was hit, healed greatly during the *QE2*'s trip home (*Southern Newspapers plc, Southampton*)

replenish the RFAs as they themselves became short of stores. A thin layer of snow that had fallen on the decks of the *QE2* soon became slush under busy feet and, as if to relieve the tension, some of the younger members of the crew exchanged snowballs with the troops as they disembarked.

Ship's boats from the *QE2* helped to tranship the Gurkhas to the *Norland* and although Phil Rentall was sorry to see them go — 'They had been courteous, obedient and efficient' — he did not relish the chances of those who were likely to oppose them on the field of battle. On the return trip from the *Norland* the small motor launch carried some of the *Ardent* survivors. Grim-faced and dressed in a motley of borrowed clothing, they kept their silence, reflecting perhaps on their recent experience of battle. Along with the survivors from other ships they were soon to revive their spirits on the trip home.

Stores were 'vert-repped' from the *QE2* to the *Norland* and *Canberra* during the day — that is, vertically replenished (lifted off by helicopter) — and a never-ending stream of supplies was lifted from deep inside the ship to both flight decks. Some stores had travelled all the way from Southampton stowed on the *QE2*'s upper decks, including several Land-Rovers, trailers and dozens of steel drums carrying oil and aviation fuel. The helicopters themselves used kerosene as fuel and the Cunard wags on the bridge had elicited feigned indignation from their naval counterparts by referring to these aircraft as 'paraffin pigeons'. Exposed as these fuel drums were it was additionally fortunate that the liner had not been strafed by enemy planes. The prevailing mainly overcast weather conditions carried with them protection from inquisitive or aggressive Argentinian aircraft but the hours spent at anchor were anxious as she was still not invulnerable to lurking submarines. Sentries stood continuously by their automatic weapons, constantly scanning the entrance to the bay and the sky below the cloud-line, but the ship remained unmolested.

The *Canberra* — 'The Great White Whale' as she had become known — took on her troops from the shuttle trawlers and the tug *Typhoon*. The 1st Welsh Guards, 2nd Scots Guards, HQ Land Forces Falkland Islands and many other units had been embarking

146

on the P & O liner since just after midnight, except for a break in the early hours. Just before 3pm HMS *Leeds Castle* came along *Canberra*'s port side to take off the rest of the *Ardent* survivors and forty minutes later the Royal Marines Band, whose numbers act as stretcher bearers during times of conflict, played during the survivors' disembarkation. As the *Castle* left the *Canberra*'s side, *Ardent*'s crew broke into the 'Oggie' chant beloved of British Service personnel — and rugby players — everywhere. The 'Oi! Oi! Oi!' response burst from the entire ship's cheering company lining *Canberra*'s rails and *Ardent*'s crew responded with applause, grateful for the loving care that *Canberra* had given them since their ordeal; they then watched her in silence as they left her side and until they could see her no more.

Cross-decking and storing the *Canberra* came to a halt just before 7pm, the remaining stores on deck would subsequently be off-loaded on to trawlers during the night. The *QE2*'s helicopters were also transferred to the *Canberra* and secured on board.

Some of the *Canberra*'s crew wondered why they, and not the *QE2*, were going back to the war zone; was it perhaps because of their battle experience, or because their ship was more manoeuvrable than the *QE2* in the confined waters around the Falklands, or was it because of the past difficulties that the Cunarder had had with her engines and which might let her down again? Anyway, *Canberra* was to go back and later that evening she weighed anchor. By the next morning she and the *Norland* had gone, leaving a bay occasionally misted by showers of sleet and snow.

During the day a group of men from the *QE2* went ashore to liaise with the troops guarding the island and to have a look round. The old whaling station looked forlorn with its broken-windowed, wooden buildings and the derelict whaling ships keeling over at their jetty. The men had been warned not to enter any of the buildings just in case these were still booby-trapped, but a group did go into the church, which was built in 1813, and amazed unwary passers-by with a spirited rendering of Bach's 'Toccata and Fugue in D' on the old, hand-pumped organ. The damaged, captured Argentinian submarine, *Santa Fe*, lay sunk alongside a jetty with a notice painted on her listing conning tower declaring that she was 'Out of bounds to all personnel'. Some of the shore-based troops were taken back to the *QE2* for lunch in conditions of sharp contrast to those of their quarters ashore.

The RFA *Stromness* had meanwhile arrived in the bay with *Coventry* survivors and these boarded the liner; in turn, the *Stromness* received some of the supplies that the *Canberra* had not been able to wait for, and 400 troops.

As the troops had left the *QE2* (cleaning boot and pack marks from cabin walls before departing) for the next stage of their journey, the liner's crew had been saddened by their departure. Friends had been made on both sides and crewmembers were later to feel proud as tales of the Brigade's exploits became known. They were even more saddened when they heard of the Brigade's losses, especially so when thirty-three of the Welsh Guards that they had carried died when the LSL (Landing Ship Logistic) *Sir Galahad* was bombed and set on fire in Bluff Cove on 9 June. Photographs of the resulting conflagration and rescue became, for many, amongst the most dramatic and heroic pictures of the entire war.

During the troop disembarkation, Bob Bantock had taken leave of his life-long pal who had joined the Scots Guards and wondered whether he would see him again. He did not hear from him for several months after the war had finished until, in the small-hours of the morning at a disco in Brighton, as the National Anthem was being played, he spotted the young Guardsman standing to attention amongst the crowd in the middle of the floor; and so the two friends were unexpectedly reunited.

By the afternoon of 29 May the situation in Cumberland Bay had visibly changed. A report had been received by the *QE2* that a fleet-support tanker that kept the RFA tankers 'topped-up' was being bombed a few hundred miles away. This was the STUFT *British Wye*, a 25,000-ton tanker that, in peaceful days, belonged to British Petroleum. An apparent air threat seemed to be closing in on the *QE2* and the rapidly deteriorating weather conditions, that in the afternoon caused the barometer to drop and brought in a Force 6 from the north-west, convinced her captain that it was time to leave.

There were still stores and ammunition in the holds but it was decided that the ship's safety overweighed any requirement for these items. The ship started to yaw in the increasing swell and the embarkation platforms at the aft ends of the boat deck (normally used as stepping-off platforms, when lowered to 5 Deck, for cruise passengers disembarking on shore excursions) were damaged by the trawlers coming heavily alongside in the swell.

So, with the survivors of the *Coventry, Ardent* and *Antelope* safely on board, the engines were put on 'Stand By' just after 4pm. When hatches were secured and cranes stowed, heaving commenced on the anchor cable at 5.10 but the anchor was not finally lifted and stowed until fifteen minutes later after the *Junella* had left the ship's side at 5.20 with the last 60 men. By now there was a full gale blowing. Engine revolutions built up to 100rpm and then 140rpm as the *QE2* passed Banff Point. Two hours later the ship was once more in the ice region; many of these bergs had been broken from South Georgia's own glaciers. Revolutions were reduced to 100rpm. The passages through the ice were later described by Captain Peter Jackson as 'harrowing'. Shortly after 11am the *QE2* passed the last of the icebergs and the officer of the watch had the rare experience of watching one of them slowly turn over in the water. Black-out was also in force and the only signs that an ocean liner was carefully navigating an ice-field were the sounds of the wind caused by her passing intermingled with the broken noises of the waves and a distant throb of engines.

The *QE2* was safe and unscathed. It was now assumed on board that the survivors from the sinkings were to be landed at Ascension and that the liner would then return to South Georgia or even to the Total Exclusion Zone around the Falklands to act as an accommodation ship or whatever else was required of her.

By late evening of 29 May the ice-field was cleared and the weather remained fine and clear. The following day brought about a change in time as clocks were regulated to Greenwich Mean Time minus one hour, and the weather deteriorated as the wind increased to Force 8 from WNW — the liner rolled heavily in rough seas and she shipped water over the bow.

Late afternoon of 1 June, notice was given that the *QE2*, down to her last 1,000 tonnes of fuel, would rendezvous with the Royal Fleet Auxiliary *Bayleaf* shortly after 8am the next morning; this was duly done and the fuel-replenishment line was connected at 9am. Before the rendezvous, however, the *QE2* had been feeling the effects of the very rough sea. The stabilisers could not cope with the existing sea state causing two drums of hydrochloric acid to break loose and which had to be secured. A change of course was made and the stabilisers retracted to help improve the *QE2*'s sea-keeping qualities. The sea was still rough and both ships heaved as nearly 4,000 tonnes of high-grade naval 'Dieso' fuel passed from the *Bayleaf*, which was on her maiden trip, to the *QE2*. The liner's engineers thought that they might as well top up with naval fuel as it was of a better quality than the fuel they normally used and it was 'free'! The fuelling took a very long time — just over nine and a half hours; just before 7pm the line, which was showing signs of chaffing, was returned to the *Bayleaf* which then took her leave of the *QE2*.

As the ship sailed north many of the crew did their best to make the *Coventry*, *Ardent* and *Antelope* survivors feel secure. At first their efforts went unrewarded and they met a great deal of reticence, but gradually the men of the Royal Navy realised that they were amongst friends and men of their own sort. Brian Atkinson, a machine maintainer, was told by a group of sailors that, although they had joined a fighting service, nobody had really thought that they would actually be needed in action. One young survivor had been in his quarters on his ship when she was hit. The ensuing fireball tore through the ship and the young man and his brother helped one of their mates, who had an injured arm, out through a hatch to safety. They were the only survivors from that area. As the days went on the sailors wanted to talk more and more about their experiences and eventually became glad to have sympathetic listeners. In spite of all their trials the survivors agreed that they would like to get on to similar ships to the ones that they had lost and with the same crews, as far as possible, as, to them, their ships were their families. The more seriously injured were put into the first-class cabins where, with proper rest and attention, their condition improved as the *QE2* steamed towards Ascension. The captain of HMS *Coventry*, Captain David Hart-Dyke, who received facial injuries when his ship was rocked by explosions, was amongst those with their own room.

Although there was now more rapport between the Cunarder's crew and the service personnel on board than there had been on the trip south, naval discipline still prevailed and physical exercises were held each morning. The sailors were to remain in their own ship's companies until they disembarked. A rather ribald show, a 'Sod's Opera', was organised and performed by the naval party and the crew, including the women, enjoyed it thoroughly. The crew had also delved into their own possessions and had kitted the survivors out in a variety of clothes which made a change from the white overalls that some of them had been given by the *Canberra*'s crew.

On 3 June it was heard that the *Queen Elizabeth 2* was to proceed direct to Southampton and disembark the survivors there. The news was met with mixed feelings as the Cunard crew had anticipated going 'back down', but they had accomplished what they had set out to do, and more. The 629 survivors were, however, glad to be going north — especially on such a ship as this, although, some said, they would have preferred to be going home on their own ship. The same day a naval mess dinner was held by the Royal Naval officers for the officers of the *QE2*. Instead of the usual splendid mess dress the officers wore whatever they had been given but the patriotism expressed in the speeches and the liveliness of the after-dinner games showed that the Navy had not been cowed by events. If anything, they would have loved to go back to the South Atlantic for another go. The voyage north had revived many a sunken spirit and the men were glad of it.

The liner was now in better weather; the weather she had experienced as she left Cumberland Bay had been the prelude to many days of very rough conditions as the winter in the South Atlantic took a hold. By 4 June she was once again near Ascension and the *Dumbarton Castle*, still in her guise as a guard ship to the island and as a dispatch vessel, met the *QE2* at mid-afternoon. Helicopters arrived from Ascension and 'vert-repping' commenced with the *Castle*, ammunition amongst other items being off-loaded from the liner.

These were some of the stores that had returned from South Georgia, where there had been no time to unload. Several SAS men, survivors from a crashed helicopter who had been taken on at Cumberland Bay, disembarked here so as to avoid the publicity awaiting in Southampton. By 6.15pm, flying operations were concluded and, with her engines increasing revolutions to 140rpm, the *QE2* headed for home.

Just after a bright midday on 5 June, the ship was ploughing through a moderate sea with a low swell at just under 24 knots. At 6.30pm those on board felt safe from the aggression of the past several days and the radar was switched on.

The days passed on board with the survivors improving in both mind and spirit, thanks to the sympathy and care that they received from the ship's crew, and undoubtedly an occasional beer! Boat drills were held, as on the voyage down, but the surviving naval officers were anxious that the plans should work in practice and not just in theory, recent events bringing home to them the necessity for efficient evacuation.

Excitement in Britain was reaching a crescendo and preparations were being made to welcome the *QE2* home. As she was to be the first arrival from the war zone, the public was eager to express its appreciation and the reception that she was to be given would release the feelings of relief in a spectacular way. Cunard themselves had been caught slightly off-guard by the liner's homecoming as they were unaware that she was on her way back to them until after she had passed Ascension Island. Bernard Crisp, Cunard's UK director had been told at breakfast-time on 6 June. Arrangements were made to start inspecting the liner almost as soon as she docked so that assessments could be made of the work that had to be carried out in reconverting her to civilian life. Initially this would include removal of the heli-pads and other work to bring her up to a cruising standard, all paid for by the Ministry of Defence, but Cunard also wanted rearrangements of some of the public rooms to make the liner more competitive in the cruising world.

To honour the ship, her crew and the cargo of survivors that she bore, Her Majesty Queen Elizabeth the Queen Mother requested that she meet the *QE2* as the liner sailed through the Solent *en route* to Southampton. So, on 10 June, the *QE2* prepared to receive stores via helicopter as she neared the approaches to the English Channel. From Culdrose in Cornwall, helicopters flew out to meet her as she reached Mount's Bay and in the late afternoon she received supplies of naval kit for the sailors, advances of compensation and pay for each man, several VIPs (including one who would debrief the crew and survivors and tell them what they could — and could not — say to the media) and, most welcome of all, a batch of Cornish pasties — the 'oggie' of the famous chant — that had been sent out as a welcoming gesture by the manufacturers.

To facilitate the meeting with the Royal Yacht *Britannia* bearing the Queen Mother the next morning and in order to arrive in Southampton at a suitable time, the *QE2* had her speed reduced throughout the night, steaming at between 60–80rpm. The next day, as she steamed along the Dorset coast, she passed HMS *Londonderry* which fired a salute in honour of a Cunard Queen that had, like her predecessors, proved herself in war by helping to shorten a conflict by her troop-carrying capacity.

By 6.30am on 11 June the ship's company was called to flying stations as, during the course of the morning, helicopters would be landing on her flight decks bringing, amongst others Admiral Sir John Fieldhouse (C-in-C Fleet) and Lord Matthews who came aboard to talk to the survivors and crew. They were to give a press conference whilst still on board to forty pressmen also flown out, who later climbed to every advantageous position to record the *QE2*'s triumphant return.

By 9am the familiar sight of the red-and-white Needles lighthouse could be seen at the base of the most seaward of the chalk mounds that protrude from the western tip of the Isle of Wight. This marks the entrance to the Solent, that haven of international yachtsmen, and the start of a victorious procession towards Southampton.

A message was received by the captain from the Queen Mother:

I am pleased to welcome you back as *QE2* returns to home waters after your tour of duty in the South Atlantic. The exploits of your own ship's company and the deeds of valour of those who served in *Antelope, Coventry* and *Ardent* have been acclaimed throughout the land and I am glad to add my personal tribute.

Captain Jackson replied on behalf of the ship and those on board: 'Please convey to Her Majesty Queen Elizabeth our thanks for her kind message. Cunard's *Queen Elizabeth 2* is proud to have been of service to Her Majesty's Forces.'

As the *QE2* sailed serenely by the Needles she was met by the first of what was to become a huge accompanying flotilla of small craft, the occupants of which waved to anyone on the liner and were waved to in return. Helicopters and light aircraft circled above and a jet fighter roared over in salute. From every vantage point between the Needles and Cowes on the Isle of Wight and along the Hampshire coast people came in their thousands to witness the triumphant return.

Off Cowes, the Royal Yacht *Britannia* was waiting, her bow pointing towards Portsmouth. As the *QE2* prepared to pass along off the yacht's port side, the battle-survivors lined the liner's heli-pads. One hundred and seventy-seven men from the *Ardent* stood to attention on the forward flight deck whilst 255 from the *Coventry* and 197 from the *Antelope* lined the aft heli-pad in true naval order. The Cunard crew lined the Boat Deck and the fore part of the superstructure. A band of the Royal Marines on board the *Britannia* struck up 'Britannia Rules the Waves' and, after giving Her Majesty three cheers, the survivors broke into 'Land of Hope and Glory'. The figure of the Queen Mother, dressed in her favourite blue, could clearly be seen on the yacht, waving to the men on board the liner — and to the ship herself. The *QE2* sent Her Majesty another signal as they passed each other in the warm and breezy sunshine: 'Please convey to Her Majesty Queen Elizabeth, with humble duty the Master, Officers and Ratings of the Royal and Merchant Navies embarked in *QE2*, join in offering their loyal greetings.' As the liner left the Royal Yacht behind she saluted her well-wisher with a sonorous signal from her siren.

Still the people on the shore cheered and waved and a huge crowd, having gathered at Cowes, watched as the *QE2* turned to port preparing to navigate the curving channel that led into Southampton Water. The survivors had prepared their own banners; *Coventry*'s men held up one that said 'HMS *Coventry* — Rule Britannia' painted around a map of the Falklands and the men from *Ardent*, hoping for

154

a victory of a different sort, sported a banner proclaiming — 'Falklands First, World Cup Next!'

The liner was now being escorted by tugs that had joined her just before 11am to help her in berthing. Tugs of the Red Funnel Group were in attendance with the *Albert* (the little boat that had helped the crippled *QE2* down Southampton Water when she had left England almost four weeks before) and the *Culver* at the bow, and the *Ventnor*, *Chale* and the larger *Calshot* stationed aft.

The *QE2* reached the Calshot light vessel and once more turned to port to come in line with the port of Southampton and into the sight of those thousands waiting excitedly on the Dock Head. To them she still looked a small dark ship in the distance; to those on the island shores and on the Royal Yacht she now presented a broadside profile, gleaming in the early summer sun. Slowly she progressed past the sandy promontory of Calshot Spit until she disappeared from the view of the island spectators, behind the trees of the New Forest. She passed by the Fawley Oil Refinery and the tankers at berth there greeted her with blasts on their throaty sirens, to which the liner responded, sending the air vibrating with the depth of her call. Smaller craft too, kept calling her with their tooting and received the customary three blasts in return.

The crowd on Southampton's Dock Head was at a fever pitch of excitement. Union Jacks, both large and small, fluttered from waving arms. A band of the Royal Marines marched to and fro playing patriotic airs and the electric atmosphere was communicated even to those who knew no one on board but were there just to see the ship safely home. The water around the *QE2* became white with foam generated by the hundreds of pleasure craft, tugs, yachts and police craft that darted around the ocean giant. Occasionally a yell of delight would burst forth as a spectator recognised a loved one on board. The men waved wildly from the decks in response and their relief was sometimes shown in tears.

The liner sedately, but painfully slowly it seemed, passed by berths 38 and 39 where she would shortly dock. She progressed a little further upstream and then, at 11.17am, allowed the tugs to coerce her gently round to starboard until she was facing down-

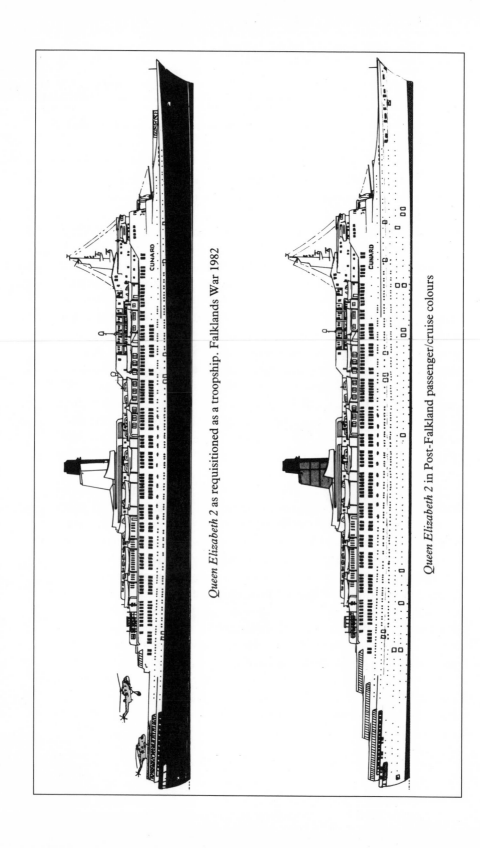

Queen Elizabeth 2 as requisitioned as a troopship. Falklands War 1982

Queen Elizabeth 2 in Post-Falkland passenger/cruise colours

stream. Thirteen minutes later the manoeuvre was complete but it was another quarter of an hour before she was alongside and the first line was thrown ashore. By midday, on Friday 11 June, the *QE2* was secure, safe and home.

Relatives of the injured were allowed on board first. Of all the injured taken on at Grytviken only seven remained in the ship's hospital and only one had to be hospitalised on his return — a great credit to the care that they had received. The multitude of banners were lowered as the first of the survivors came ashore, walking down a red carpet to the tune of 'Hearts of Oak', to tearful and joyful reunions on the quayside and more private reunions in the privacy of the dock terminal.

The *QE2* had done her job well. A period of refurbishment now awaited her during several weeks in dry dock.

It was expected that, although much of her cruising timetable had been disrupted, she would benefit from the publicity generated by her days as a troopship. This proved to be a correct assumption, as she was fully booked for her first post-Falklands trip on 14 August.

After the refit the *QE2* had changed. Now she bore the mark of a real Cunarder — her funnel, originally painted black with a white casing, had been painted in the traditional Cunard deep orange with black top and two black horizontal bands. (These stripes were, however, each composed of two widths of 4-in black tape which became unstuck to flap in the wind after three or four voyages.) The biggest surprise, however, was that she now had a light pebble-grey hull. This proved to be unpopular with the crew and the general public — it was said to be Lord Matthews' idea — and thankfully she was repainted as a Cunard Queen should be with her original dark hull.

The *QE2* often appears in the news for many reasons, but the fact remains that she has proved the worth of Britain retaining a passenger fleet capable of deep and rough sea voyaging. Many cruise liners have been built over the past decade but these are lightly built ships intended for tropical seas and their value as troopships in any future conflict — and the possibility of one, on however large or small a scale, cannot be denied — is open to doubt. The *QE2* should therefore be regarded as the last of the super-liners and will undoubtedly be included in the list of famous liners that have helped their country in times of crisis and made their own contribution to true liberty, not least of which are the *Queen Mary* and *Queen Elizabeth*. Long may she sail.

Appendix

Service units carried aboard the *QE2* from Southampton to South Georgia, May 1982.

Royal Navy Party 1980
Headquarters Land Forces Falkland Islands
5 Infantry Brigade comprising:
    4th Field Regiment Royal Artillery (97 Field Battery)
    Blowpipe Troop 43 Air Defence Battery
    32 Guided Weapons Regiment Royal Artillery
    9 Parachute Squadron Royal Engineers
    5 Infantry Brigade HQ and Signals Squadron
    2nd Battalion The Scots Guards
    1st Battalion The Welsh Guards
    1st Battalion the 7th Duke of Edinburgh's Own Gurkha Rifles
    656 Squadron Army Air Corps
    407 Troop Royal Corps of Transport
    16 Field Ambulance Royal Army Medical Corps
    81 Ordnance Company Royal Army Ordnance Corps
    10 Field Workshops Royal Electrical and Mechanical Engineers
    5 Infantry Brigade Platoon of 160 Provost Company Royal Military Police
    8 Field Cash Office Royal Army Pay Corps
    81 Intelligence Section
    601 Tactical Air Control Party
    602 Tactical Air Control Party

Bibliography

Armstrong, Warren. *Atlantic Highway* (George G. Harrap & Company Limited, 1961)

Bisset, Sir James. *Commodore: War, Peace and Big Ships* (Angus & Robertson Limited, 1961)

Bonsor, N. R. P. *North Atlantic Seaway* (T. Stephenson & Sons Limited, Prescot Lancashire, 1955)

Braynard, Frank O. *Lives of the Liners* (Cornell Maritime Press, New York, 1947)

Braynard, Frank O. & Miller, William H. *Fifty Famous Liners* (Patrick Stephens Limited, Cambridge, 1982)

Brinnin, John Malcolm. *The Sway of the Grand Saloon* (Delacorte Press, New York, 1971)

Coleman, Terry. *The Liners* (G. P. Putnam's Sons, New York, 1977)

Cronican, Frank & Mueller, Edward, A. *The Stateliest Ship* (The Steamship Historical Society of America, New York, 1968)

Dodman, Frank E. *Ships of the Cunard Line* (Adlard Coles Limited, 1955)

Eisele, Peter (ed). *Steamboat Bill* (journal, 1966–1983) (The Steamship Historical Society of America, New York)

Fox, Robert. *Eye-witness, Falklands* (Methuen London Ltd, 1982)

Hanrahan, Brian & Fox, Robert. *I Counted Them All Out and I Counted Them All Back* (BBC Publications, 1982)

Harding, Steve. *Grey Ghost* (Pictorial Histories Publishing Company, Missoula, Montana, 1982)

Hastings, Max & Jenkins, Simon. *Battle of the Falklands* (Michael Joseph, 1983)

Hyde, Francis E. *Cunard and the North Atlantic 1840–1973* (The Macmillan Press Limited, 1975)

Kitson, Linda. *The Falklands War — A Visual Diary* (Mitchell Beazley International Limited & Imperial War Museum, 1982)

Lacey, Robert. *The Queens of the North Atlantic* (Sidgwick & Jackson Limited, 1973)

McGuire, Joseph B. *The Sea My Surgery* (William Heinemann Limited, 1957)

MacLean, Commodore Donald. *Queen's Company* (Hutchinson & Company, 1965)

BIBLIOGRAPHY

Maxtone-Graham, John. *The Only Way to Cross* (USA) and as *The North Atlantic Run* (UK) (The Macmillan Company, New York; Cassell & Company Limited, both 1972)

Mitchell, W. H. & Robinson, Nigel. *The Cunard Line, A Post-war History* (Marinart Limited, Deal, Kent, 1975)

P & O Steam Navigation Company. *Canberra — The Great White Whale Goes to War* (1982)

Potter, Neil & Frost, Jack. *The Mary, The Inevitable Ship* (George G. Harrap & Company Limited, 1961)

Potter, Neil & Frost, Jack. *The Elizabeth* (George G. Harrap & Company Limited, 1965)

Potter, Neil & Frost, Jack. *Queen Elizabeth 2 — The Authorised Story* (George G. Harrap & Company Limited, 1969)

Rentall, Phillip (RNR). Unpublished manuscript — *Personal Reflections of the First Officer, QE2, During the Falklands Campaign*

Stevens, Leonard A. *The Elizabeth, The Passage of a Queen* (Alfred A. Knopf, New York, 1968)

Villar, Roger. *Merchant Ships at War* (Conway Maritime Press, 1984)

Wall, Robert. *Ocean Liners* (E. P. Dutton, New York, 1977)

Williams, David & de Kerbrech, Richard P. *Damned By Destiny* (Teredo Books Limited, Brighton, 1982)

The Cunard–White Star Quadruple-Screw Liner Queen Mary (Bonanza Books, New York, 1979)

The Queen Elizabeth (Winchester Publications Limited, 1948)

Notes on Sources

The authors would like to make special mention of the superb and illuminating information found in several books during their recent researches for *Transatlantic Liners at War*. Their respective publishers and the dates of publication may be found in the Bibliography.

Particularly helpful were the three fine histories of the Queens written by Neil Potter and Jack Frost: *The Mary, the Inevitable Ship*, *The Elizabeth* and *QE2, The Authorised Story*. The memoirs of two Cunard commodores were most impressive and valuable: Sir James Bisset's *Commodore: War, Peace and Big Ships* and Donald MacLean's *Queen's Company*. Also most useful were Terry Coleman's *The Liners*, Steve Harding's new *Grey Ghost* (specifically about the MARY during the War), Robert Lacey's *The Queens of the North Atlantic*, John Maxtone-Graham's *The Only Way to Cross*, Joseph B. McGuire's *The Sea My Surgery*, Leonard Stevens' *The Elizabeth, The Passage of a Queen* and *The Cunard-White Star Quadruple-Screw Liner 'Queen Mary'*.

For the QE2 and the Falklands conflict, mention must be made of *Merchant Ships at War* by Captain Roger Villar, *Canberra — The Great White Whale Goes to War* by Peninsular & Oriental Steam Navigation Company, *The Falklands War* by Linda Kitson and special mention and thanks to Phil Rentall for use of his, as yet unpublished, manuscript documenting his experiences as First Officer of the *Queen Elizabeth 2* during her duties as a troopship.

All of these titles were invaluable and without them this work would not have been possible.

Acknowledgements

The authors wish to thank all of those who have participated in this project. Special mention and highest appreciation goes to Captain Peter Jackson for contributing the Foreword and to Frank O. Braynard, a master among maritime historians and a constant source of new and fresh photographs. He happily offered the use of his vast collection on the Queens as well. Other very important items, such as books, brochures, press clippings and photographs, came from George Devol and the World Ocean & Cruise Society, Robert Lenzer, Ralph L. O'Hara, Steve Harding, Everett Viez and the World Ship Society, Port of New York and Southampton Branches. Further assistance and co-operation was offered by Erwin Abele, Wally Adams, Ernest Arroyo, Captain Eric Ashton-Irvine, Brian Atkinson, Robert Bantock, Frank Bilek, Norman Blundell, R. Bruce-Grice, Ralph L. Carver, J. Currie, Hugh O'Donnell, Frank Duffy, Joseph Fencil, Ralph Freeman, Barney Gallagher, John Gleason, E. R. Greenman, K. Hainsworth, Brenton Jenkins, Horst Kessler, Anthony Keasbey, Phillip Levin, Margaret Lewis, W. A. Masson, N. L. McKellar, R. M. Mills, Denis Money, Edward Neighbour, Neil Osborne and Susan Alpert at Cunard in New York City, Betty Poole, Phillip Rentall (First Officer *QE2*), Donald A. R. Reynolds, Victor Scrivens, H. Taylor, Charles F. Trapp, R. S. Trout, Willie and Marie Tinnemeyer, Cedric Wasser and Captain R. A. Woodall of the Cunard Line and many, many more who kindly co-operated with information which helped to put flesh on the bones of history. Organisations which have assisted include the Cunard Line, the Imperial War Museum in London, the *New York Times*, the Port Authority of New York & New Jersey, the Portsmouth *News*, Royal Caribbean Cruise Lines, the *Southern Evening Echo*, Southampton Central Library, Southampton Maritime Museum (especially Miss Skippings), the Steamship Historical Society and the parent World Ship Society. Warmest thoughts and appreciation to our families and friends for their inspiration and, of course, to David & Charles (Publishers) Limited for suggesting the title.

Index